Strabane Barony

during the

Ulster Plantation

1607–1641

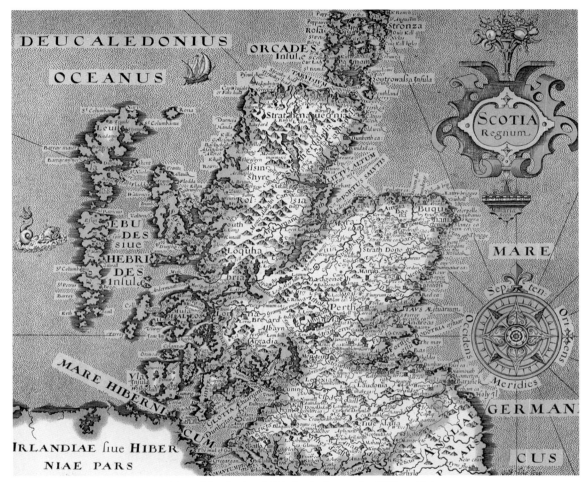

Map of Scotland *c.* 1607, *Scotia Regnum* by William Hole,
courtesy of the R.J. Hunter Collection

Strabane Barony

during the

Ulster Plantation

1607–1641

Edited by
Robert J. Hunter

ULSTER HISTORICAL FOUNDATION

Published in association with the R.J. Hunter Committee.
The Committee works to acknowledge the contribution R.J. Hunter made to the
study of our past by making more widely known the results of his research, as well
as giving limited support to others engaged in associated endeavours.

COVER DESIGN:
Bodley map for Strabane barony of 1609 and John Speed's map of Ulster *c.* 1616,
both courtesy of the Cardinal Tomás Ó Fiaich Memorial Library and Archive;
ruin of Mountcastle, near Dunnamanagh, courtesy of William Roulston.
Cover design by David Graham

First published in this format 2011
by Ulster Historical Foundation,
49 Malone Road, Belfast BT9 6RY
www.ancestryireland.com
www.booksireland.org.uk

ISBN: 978-1-903688-95-3

Printed by Industrias Gráficas Castuera
Design by FPM Publishing

Contents

Maps and Illustrations

The Place of Paisley: Scottish home of the Hamiltons, Earls of Abercorn

Foreword

FOUR HUNDRED YEARS AGO MY ANCESTOR James Hamilton, 1st Earl of Abercorn, stepped off a boat from Scotland to begin a new life in Ireland. That he should have left the comforts of a life in Scotland and all the privileges that went with his position shows something of the power of persuasion possessed by his king, James VI and I, as well as perhaps something of his own sense of adventure. He made his home at Strabane and four centuries later my family still lives in this area. This book tells his story and that of many others in this fascinating period of our history.

It was my pleasure to meet R.J. 'Bob' Hunter on more than one occasion and I was struck by his passion for history and his enthusiasm for communicating it to others. He had an inquisitive mind for all things relating to the Ulster Plantation and enjoyed excursions to early seventeenth-century castles as much as delving into the archives and exploring the documentation of the time.

I commend this book as an excellent example of the way in which a professional historian and his students can successfully work together to produce a high-quality publication. All of us can learn something from it as we look back from the vantage point of 2011 on events that changed our province forever.

JAMES ABERCORN
His Grace the Duke of Abercorn KG

Preface

THIS PROJECT DEVELOPED OUT OF AN EVENING COURSE conducted by me in Strabane under the auspices of the extra-mural department of Magee University College on the Plantation in Ulster as a whole. Afterwards, in the winters 1969–70 to 1971–2, a small group was assembled, meeting in the Abercorn Arms hotel, to make a study of the plantation in the Strabane area which we hoped would be adequate for reproduction and local sale. Since the plantation was organised on a regional basis, the barony of Strabane – allocated to Scots – formed a coherent unit of investigation. It was my function (however casually fulfilled) to attempt to provide some guidance in the use of source materials and to get together by transcript and photocopy relevant extracts from unpublished sources.

We were fortunate to secure the co-operation of Mr K.W. Nicholls of University College, Cork who provided us at a very early stage with a most valuable section on the Gaelic back ground of the Strabane region. Equally, Professor M. Perceval-Maxwell of McGill University, Montreal generously provided material on the Scottish background to plantation and on the Scottish 'undertakers' who received grants of estates in Strabane barony, prior to the publication of his own book in 1973.

Apart from their contributions and my own chapter on the town of Strabane and some additional material, the finished production is essentially the work of the Strabane Local History Group.

The contributions were written mainly during the period 1970–74. The group became disrupted in the mid 1970s and credit for much of the editorial work and the drive towards completion must go to Mr Michael Cox whose very fine maps, finished in 1978, deserve particular scrutiny. Regrettably, pressure of space has precluded footnotes, but the principal sources used are listed in the bibliography.

At the end of each section or chapter the initials of each contributor are given as follows:

> The professionals –
> > Robert J. Hunter (RJH)
> > Michael Perceval-Maxwell (MP-M)
> > Kenneth Nicholls (KN)
>
> The amateurs –
> > J. Michael Cox (JMC)
> > Mrs E. Mehaffy (Mrs M)
> > Mrs B. McGillian (Mrs McG)
> > Ian Wallace (IW)

I am very happy to record our gratitude, in the first instance, to Professor E. Rhodes, former Head of Extra-Mural Studies, Magee University College, who initially promoted the project and now to Professor A. Rogers of the Institute of Continuing Education at Magee who has been most helpful in every way in facilitating its publication. The group wishes also to acknowledge the assistance and advice of the staffs of the Public Record Office of Northern Ireland and of the then Tyrone County Library. We are particularly indebted to the Duke of Abercorn, the Public Record Office of Northern Ireland and The Board of Trinity College, Dublin for permission to reproduce the manuscripts which form the illustrations.

R.J. HUNTER
December 1981

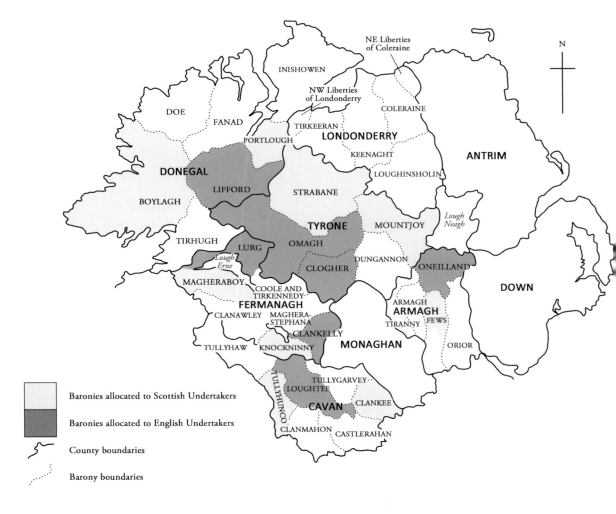

Map showing allocation of lands to English and Scottish undertakers
in the Plantation scheme of 1610

Introduction

DURING ELIZABETH'S REIGN THE POPULATION of England outgrew the resources of the country. Colonisation became one of the principal means by which this pressure was reduced. The New World was a long way off, whilst Ireland offered opportunities much closer to home. Only the area around Dublin – the Pale – was controlled directly. A plan to colonise Munster was embarked upon with mixed results. Ulster was still the main stronghold of Gaelic Ireland with the two families, O'Neill and O'Donnell, owning or controlling over half the province (the present counties of Tyrone, Londonderry and Donegal). In the east of Ulster the English had developed associations with the principal families and there had been forts around the coast since Norman times.

At the end of the 16th century the policy of 'divide and rule' was established. This in effect saw the setting up of forts on the Foyle continuing towards Ballyshannon, so attempting to divide the O'Neills (Tyrone) from the O'Donnells (Donegal). Forts were established at Greencastle (a Norman site), Culmore, Derry, Dunalong and Lifford. Alliances were made with some of the minor Gaelic leaders such as Niall Garbh O'Donnell at Castlefinn. At the same time the Elizabethan policy to 'convert' Ireland to Protestantism had been directed towards west Ulster by James I (VI of Scotland) after he ascended the English throne in 1603.

The appointment of George Montgomery as Bishop of Derry, Raphoe and Clogher followed in 1605. He started to claim upwards of half Hugh O'Neill's and Rory O'Donnell's lands for the Church. The Earl of Tyrone had also fallen out with his principal vassal in the north – Sir Donnell O'Cahan. This led to a summons by the King in 1607 to O'Neill to go to London.

Hugh O'Neill, Earl of Tyrone (d. 1616)

Suspecting that he would be imprisoned, O'Neill together with O'Donnell and upwards of sixty relatives and servants sailed to exile on the Continent. This left Gaelic Ulster leaderless and presented the opportunity for another colonisation scheme – the Plantation of Ulster.

1
Strabane barony
at the end
of the 16th century

Our survey starts well before the Plantation. Some idea of the events taking place during the ten years preceding the Flight of the Earls can be obtained from various sources, and it is important to keep in mind that there had been constant interchange of people and ideas between western Scotland and Ulster for many centuries.

Geographical background

The barony of Strabane was one of the four divisions of County Tyrone which was established in 1585; west Ulster being that part of Ireland last to be 'shired' on the English pattern for administrative purposes. It was an area of about 400 square miles, diamond-shaped with diagonal distances of 25 miles. Like all old administrative areas its boundaries are clearly defined natural features. On the west and south we find, in turn, the rivers Foyle, Finn, Fairywater (Poe Water), Strule, Camowen and Drumnakilly. To the north and east we find the Sperrin Mountains and their foothills often connected by large expanses of high moorland. The location map shows the main geographical features of the area. Above 500 feet (150 m) we usually find uncultivated or afforested bog land. The whole area has been subject to the affect of glacial activity. Most of the lower land is covered by glacial deposits of sand, gravel and clays offering differing controls to cultivation. The higher land was covered by woodlands and bogs which before the action of man would have covered well over 90% of the barony. As there is evidence

The Sperrins near Goles, Badoney parish

of man's occupation in the area going back over 5,000 years, the landscape has been moulded by this continuous settlement, which as population increased gradually altered to that seen by us today.

With varying cycles of climate change it is considered by climatologists that for the early 17th century the seasons (in the British Isles) were cooler with wetter winters than today. Occasional references to extreme conditions at that time were noted in the Calendar of State Papers. One entry for 25 March 1601 states that the 'rivers (are) in high flood, not fordable due to heavy snows now melting'. This type of weather, when linked to the fact that systematic drainage of land was unknown, would have added to the difficulties where cultivation and travelling were concerned. The controls through geographic factors would therefore be far more in evidence than today.

This geographical control on both location of settlement and of routes is very evident in Strabane barony. All the church sites and the towns of Strabane and Newtownstewart are near to or on a river bank. Both towns controlled crossing points of rivers – Strabane opposite to Lifford (known at that time as 'Liffer' or 'The Liffer') where at the time of drought and/or at low tide (the Foyle system is tidal to a point one mile above the confluence with the Finn and Mourne) the Foyle could have been forded, as was the Strule at Newtownstewart. Early routeways followed the rivers and streams or kept to non boggy land through more settled areas. Most of these have continued in use down to the present time, although it is impossible to say

An Irish chieftain feasting (from Derricke's *The Image of Irelande*)

which of the present roads, no doubt as tracks for horses, existed in the early part of the 17th century. There are occasional references to routes on old maps but they are too imprecise to be used authoritatively.

Settlements before the Plantation in Ulster were few. There would have been small groups of 'cabins' nearby the castles, churches and abbeys. The native Irish mostly lived within their family groupings – clachans. Their extent can be gauged by the spread of the 'balliboes' (named settlements), but with their division by the 17th century due to an increase in population and the pressure on land there had been a movement of population into inhospitable areas. Strabane had a settlement of modest size by 1600. When Agnes Campbell came from the Western Isles to marry Turlough Luineach O'Neill in 1569 she brought 1,000 men with her with the result that 60/80 families of Scottish descent were to be found at Strabane at the end of the century. By 1600 the English had built a series of forts along the Foyle. These included Culmore, Derry, Dunalong and Lifford, with less important ones at Castlefinn and near Newtownstewart under the jurisdiction of the principal Irish families professing or offering support to the English.

Caricature of Turlough Luineach O'Neill

The rivers were the main routes of communication. We learn that in the first decade of the 17th century, ships of 200 tons sailed up to Dunalong whilst 'barks' of 20 tons went as far as Lifford at high tide. Three miles above Dunalong it was noted that 'the water becomes narrow with islands and is fordable in many places'. At that period (as now) the fishing of salmon was of great economic and commercial importance with the fishing rights in the hands of the Bishop of Derry. From the river a traveller in the first years of the 17th century would have seen mostly birch woodland alternating with open grasslands and bogs, with coppices on the islands. The valley was considered to have 'the richest soil of all in the North'. This open 'champagne' land extended around and beyond Strabane.

Agriculture was extensive with both pastoralism and the cultivation of crops. The Irish chiefs possessed large numbers of cattle – in 1601 the son, grandson, and cousin of Turlough Luineach each possessed two thousand head. Transhumance (booleying) was practised and although 17th-century evidence for this area would seem to be nonexistent, the fact that the practice was noted later at known sites in the Sperrins endorses the longevity of this system.

The infield/outfield cultivation system, known to have survived in hilly areas in Ulster down to the 19th century, may have disappeared from the 'champagne' country around Strabane as the Plantation developed. Again there is no direct evidence of this but with the increasing population relatively intensive cultivated areas would have been found in the Foyle Valley.

JMC

Historical background – The Irish

The earliest tribal group of whom we know in what later became the barony of Strabane were the *Ui Fiachrach* of Ardstraw, a branch of that group of peoples known as the *Airghialla,* whom the accepted genealogical tradition connected with the ruling race *Ui Neill,* but whom more probably represented that section of the ancient Uladh who submitted to the rule of the invading *Hi Neil.* By the 12th century the *Ui Fiachrach* were in decay and the last mention of the tribe as a group is the recorded death of Murchadh O'Crichain, king of *Ui Fiachrach,* in 1201.

More important in the area in the 12th and 13th centuries was that branch of the *Cineal Eoghain* section of the *Ui Neill* called the *Cineal Moain,* whose territory lay around Strabane in the district called Magh Dola, and whose chiefs were the important family of O Gailmreadaigh or O'Gormley. In 1160 the O'Gormleys are found allied with the *Ui Fiachrach* against other sections

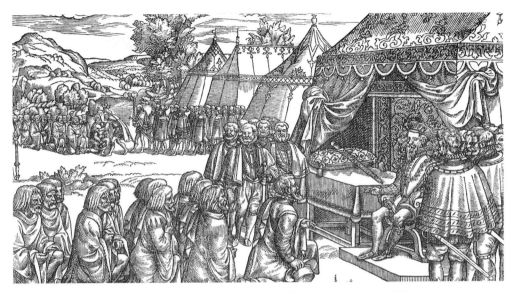

Submission of Turlough Luineach O'Neill before Lord Deputy Sidney
(from Derricke's *The Image of Irelande*)

of the *Cineal Eoghain*. The 1603 map of Ulster shows the territory of 'O'Gurmelie' in the northeast of the barony of Strabane, in the parishes of Leckpatrick and Donagheady.

The O'Neills secured the undisputed possession of the kingship of Cineal Eoghain by their defeat of the MacLachlainns at the battle of *Caimirghe* (unidentified) in 1243, and their first settlement in the Strabane region probably dates from soon after this date. In the 16th century Strabane itself with the adjacent lands was – like Dungannon and Benburb – part of the demesne lands belonging to the O'Neillship, and it seems likely that it had been occupied as such from the 13th century. No castle seems to have existed at Strabane, however, until Turlough Luineach O'Neill erected one in 1573.

The local history of the O'Neills in the Strabane region really begins with Henry Aimhreidh O'Neill (d. 1391). Henry Aimhreidh, 'the quarrelsome', whose memory was preserved in local tradition down to modern times, resided near Newtownstewart at the place where he erected a castle known in the 15th and 16th centuries as the Old Castle (*Sean-Caislean, Baile an t-sean-Caisleain*) but in more modern times, from the name of its founder, as Harry Avery's Castle.

During those two centuries many family feuds took place with varying results, which saw differing branches assuming the O'Neillship. After the death of Shane O'Neill in 1567 Turlough Luineach, one of four contenders, became the O'Neill.

In 1573 he erected for the first time a castle at Strabane on the demesne lands of the O'Neillship there, which, however, he himself demolished when the Earl of Essex made his expedition against him in September 1574, for fear that it should be occupied by the latter. After the re-establishment of peace in 1575 it was rebuilt and remained Turlough Luineach's usual residence until his death in 1595, when he was buried at Ardstraw. In 1593 Turlough Luineach resigned the O'Neillship in favour of Hugh O'Neill, Earl of Tyrone, reserving, however, during his lifetime a number of rents due by vassals and much of the demesne lands, including the lands of Strabane and Largevicnenie, and the adjacent lands from Burndennet in the north to Burndouglas in the south, and between the Finn and the Derg.

Turlough Luineach's son, Sir Art Og or Arthur O'Neill, had already in 1592 endeavoured to secure his future possession, after his father's death, not only of the lands which had belonged to his grandfather Niall Conallach, but also of Strabane itself. He seems to have successfully pleaded his cause with the government in spite of the opposition of Earl Hugh, but surprisingly enough was induced by the latter to join with him in his rising and to demolish once again, in 1598, the castle of Strabane which his father had erected. On 1 June 1600, he, however, made his submission to the Queen and was established with an English garrison at Dunalong on the Foyle below Strabane, where he died – allegedly of alcoholism – on 13 October 1600. His position as head of his sept passed to his half-brother Cormac, who with most of Sir Arthur's followers had remained in revolt and who along with them made his submission in March 1601.

A list drawn up at the time of their submission records that Cormac, his nephew Turlough (son of Sir Arthur) and his cousin Niall MacArt were each the possessors of 2,000 cows; the Sliocht Airt had 4,000 between them; O'Quin had 1,000; and three other chiefs: MacHugh, MacBrien and MacGuirke (of Termonmaguirk) 500 each; while the unfortunate O'Gormley, although formerly a rich man, had suffered for the nearness of his lands to Dunalong by the loss of his entire stock. On 1 April 1601, Cormac O'Neill received the Queen's pardon along with his wife and three sons, the seven sons of his brother Sir Arthur and others of their followers. Although he had thus submitted, Cormac was not trusted by the local English commander, Sir Henry Docwra, who offended him by putting much of Cormac's forces under the command of some of the latter's followers, whom he made directly responsible to himself, and in August 1601 Cormac again went into rebellion. He was still out in April 1603, and the last reference to his name is in April 1604, when the parish Badoney is described as lying in Cormac O'Neill's country.

After the disappearance of Cormac from the scene, the headship of the Art Og's sept devolved upon his nephew Turlough, already mentioned, who with the other subchiefs and freeholders of Tyrone was engaged in a constant struggle with Hugh, Earl of Tyrone, during the years leading up to the latter's flight in 1607. When in 1605 the Lord Deputy made a tour of Ulster and heard the complaints of the Tyrone freeholders against the Earl, who was endeavouring to dispossess them of their lands, the only exception which he made to his general policy of neutrality on the issue was to order that Turlough MacArt should have possession of one ballybetagh between the Derg and the Finn free of rent. The smallness of the allotment – although the question of the right to the remaining lands was left open – shows that the position of Niall Conallach's descendents had much declined over the preceding few years. In another few years they would be totally expelled by the Plantation.

The tract known as 'Ceart Ui Neill' names some of the other landowning families of the Strabane region. Besides the O'Gormleys, already mentioned, the Cineal Moain were represented by the families of MacConally, MacHugh, O'Devin, O'Kelly and O'Laverty. The latter two are not mentioned in the 16th– and 17th–century sources. The O'Devins must have occupied the four balliboes of Coolemunterdevin of the 1608 survey; a Jenkin O'Devin was one of the native grantees in the Plantation. The MacConallys (MacConallaidh) are probably identical with the McEnallows, fifteen of whom were pardoned as followers of Cormac O'Neill in 1601. Another family mentioned in the tract are the MacNamees (MacConmidhe), hereditary poets of the O'Neills, who were settled at a place called Loch Ui Mhaoldubhain, apparently somewhere near Ardstraw, but unidentified. Eight of them were pardoned with Cormac O'Neill. Two important families in the late 16th century not referred to in the tract were those of MacGunshenan and O'Quin. Twenty-seven MacGunshenans were pardoned with Cormac O'Neill in 1601; they included a prominent commander called Turlough Maguylson. The most numerous name among the followers of Cormac O'Neill pardoned along with him was MacConny, no less than 48 bearers of this name being listed in the Fiant of pardon.

KN

Historical background – The Scots and Scotland

It has been mentioned earlier that Scots had been living in Strabane during the latter part of the 16th century with 60/80 families resident there about 1600. During the uprising of Sir Cahir O'Dogherty they had fled to Lifford obtaining protection in the fort there. Bishop George Montgomery had recruited a number of Scots during 1607/10 to come to develop the church lands and others had made their way to the area. This included those who had settled in Lifford. Sir Richard Hansard had started to build a town there in 1607 and by 1611 there were 60 families resident, of whom a dozen were Scots.

Thus we see that by the time the Plantation started substantial numbers of Scots were known to live in the Strabane area. However in the 17th century, before a nation could send settlers abroad, it required a surplus of people and a surplus of capital. By 1610, when the main scheme for the Ulster plantation began, Scotland had both. That she was ready to embark on such schemes is shown by her efforts to establish colonies of Lowlanders on the island of Lewis in 1599 and 1605. Scotland certainly had people to spare at the beginning of the seventeenth century, which is simply another way of saying that her economy could not employ all of her inhabitants. In one decade – the 1590s – two acts of parliament had to be passed to deal with the increasing number of vagrants and beggars; the local authorities were presented with the same problem.

Contemporary opinion confirms this picture of Scotland as a country with too many people. The Venetian ambassador in London, writing in 1622, remarked that Scotland was well populated, 'the women being prolific, showing how much more fruitful are northern parts'. Quite apart from such casual remarks as this about conditions in Scotland, there is abundant evidence to show that Scots were leaving their homeland in large numbers. After James became king of England, the stream of Scots going south became an embarrassment to the English privy council, which had to ask the Scottish authorities to try to take action to stem the flow. Nor was England the only country to receive Scottish immigrants. William Lithgow who visited Poland in 1616, calculated that no less than 30,000 Scottish families had settled there.

This surplus of population can, in part, be explained by the unusual degree of political stability Scotland enjoyed after James VI attained his majority. Nobles and lairds could devote their energies to other pursuits besides feuds. As a result, it was no longer necessary for landlords to gather round them large bodies of retainers with which to attack their neighbours. Frequently, the only employment Scots could find after 1600 was military service under a foreign prince, particularly Gustavus Adolphus.

Coinciding with the freedom from political anarchy, and surely in part as a consequence of it, went a period of economic stability. Inflation had struck Scotland even harder than England during the 16th century. In 1571, the Scottish pound was worth approximately one-fifth of the pound sterling; by 1600 it had dropped in value to one-twelfth of its English counterpart. But there it remained. There is no evidence of any serious decline in the value of the Scottish pound, relative to sterling, during the remainder of James's reign. There is evidence to indicate that the country prospered during the period. In 1609, the 'tack' or rent of the customs amounted to some £76,666 (Scots). Two years later, after an upward revision of the rates, the tack rose to £120,000 (Scots). In 1616, after much competitive bidding, there was another rise to £140,000 (Scots). Without a doubt, the landlords in Scotland, whose position in society was dominant, reaped much of the benefit of this prosperity, and it was from this group that the undertakers were drawn.

MP-M

2

The Plantation

The Plan

There were three main reasons why a plantation was considered desirable. Firstly, the high cost of keeping order in Ulster (and Ireland generally) which had increased during the decade to 1607, a period in which the English had endeavoured to surround and separate the Earls of Tyrone and Tyrconnell. Secondly, the strategic need to obtain complete control over Ireland and to avoid further European conflict and involvement as had happened when the Spaniards came to the support of O'Neill in 1601 (Battle of Kinsale). Thirdly, the desire to have Ireland within the Protestant fold also pointed to a colonisation scheme linked to an English system of land tenure and an introduction of British settlers sympathetic to the Protestant cause. With the Flight of the Earls (who had been joined by Cuconnaught Maguire, owner of half Fermanagh, the overlordship of most of the present counties of Donegal, Tyrone and Fermanagh became 'vacant'. In addition County Cavan had been 'found to belong to the crown' in 1606.

Lord Deputy Chichester acted quickly to resolve the problem and to instigate a plan which would achieve a solution to the 'Irish' question. By the end of September 1607 the privy council had agreed to his proposal that most of the land be granted in small lots to Irish freeholders with the remainder going to servitors. These were soldiers and government officials who had been employed in Ireland.

The servitors would in turn bring in settlers from both England and Scotland. After O'Dogherty's rebellion had been subdued in 1608 and the crown's subsequent decision that all land held by Shane O'Neill in 1569 at the time of his attainder was to be forfeited, most of the counties of Armagh and Londonderry were added to the area available to the Plantation.

A survey was carried out in 1608 and a commission produced a report on how the Plantation should be organised. The plan was published in January 1609 and subsequently modified in the light of criticism by Chichester. The territorial arrangement was to be one in which groups of owners with a common background were to be settled in a more or less uniform way throughout the counties. There were three categories of grantees: English and Lowland Scottish undertakers (so called because of the conditions they undertook to fulfil), servitors, and Irish from the confiscated areas who were restored to some of the land. The undertakers' land was to be completely cleared of the native Irish and resettled with Scottish or English tenants whilst the servitors were allowed to have Irish tenantry, it being considered that their military experience would enable them to maintain control. The main weight of the colonisation was made the responsibility of the undertakers.

A definite attempt was made to allocate land on a proportionate basis; Scottish and English undertakers were to be granted equal amounts and their combined share was to be one and a half times as much as the servitors. Areas of the land were to be designated for the support of corporate towns and schools and each parish was to be allocated glebe land. The small areas already assigned for the support of forts was not to be reallocated and grants made to prominent Irish figures immediately before the Plantation were, where there was a definite legal title in patents, not to be disturbed. Church land, the property of or claimed by the bishops and other religious figures, was granted to the bishops of the Protestant succession whilst the monastic property was granted to lay proprietors.

RJH

The Plantation survey of Strabane barony in 1609

The commissioners appointed to survey the escheated counties left London on 21 June 1609, spent some time in Dublin, leaving there for the north on 30 July. They reached Derry on 14 August, Lifford on 17 August and Dungannon on 21 August.

The method of the survey was to call together at central points leading people of the area who described the area to the commissioners. There is no evidence to show that any consideration was given to recording the occupiers of the land. It was no doubt sufficient for government purposes, it having assumed the ownership of this part of Ulster when the principal landowners left the country in the previous year.

This survey, although an improvement on the one carried out the previous year, still left much to be desired. A fundamental error was that the surveyors had been noting Irish acres which meant that in English measure – used in the subsequent report – there was an error of about a third (see table later). Additionally, the balliboes (equivalent to the modern 'townland') recorded indicated only the extent of the cultivated and settled land in the Irish land tenure form of occupancy. There was no attempt to quantify the extent of the bog, wood or hill land. It will be shown later that in Strabane barony many balliboes had in effect been subdivided and hence the equal division of land among settlers was impossible.

Strabane barony was featured on two coloured maps. They show what is essentially freehand pictorial representation of the location of balliboes one with another and in relationship to principal rivers, with a general indication of hill land and woodland. Also featured are the castles and religious houses. These include castles or forts at Omagh, Newtownstewart, Island McHugh (Barons Court), Strabane, Lifford, Dunalong and one along the Burndennet river; churches at Camus, Glenroan, Scarvagherin and Dunmullan; and religious houses at Bunowen, Corick and at both Granges.

Almost 300 balliboes are named on the two maps which compares with just over 500 modern townlands featured amongst today's administrative units. Ninety-three out of the 133 balliboes on the map showing the north and east of the Strabane barony are easily identifiable, having the same (or virtually the same) spelling today. The precise location of 26 balliboes on the maps with non-modern names were determined during the research mostly by reference to Lodge's copies of the Records of the Rolls which list sessiogh divisions of balliboes. On the second map only 100 out of 156 balliboes bear similar or identical names to those of modern townlands. Reference to the Records of the Rolls for the area immediately to the north and south of Strabane does not help one to pinpoint precisely the location of these old balliboes. Similarly, for the lower valley of the River Derg and near to Omagh, it will be seen that in these areas there are many anglicised names on modern maps, including names of later Plantation settlers, especially around Urney.

Some areas are far better depicted than others – the areas at the greatest distance from Strabane are extremely inaccurate. The map shows all balliboes of almost equal size which of course was far from reality. Each balliboe in this area was considered to have 60 acres of profitable (usable) land. Thus the 34 balliboes to the north of the Burndennet River equals 2040 acres, say 2000 acres and was considered an appropriate area to be allocated to a 'planter'. This became the Dunalong proportion. 2,000 plantation acres was the equivalent of 3,250 statute acres. In fact Dunalong has a total of 10,350 acres. The table on page 15 shows the comparison between the 1610 plantation allocation of proportions with actual land area contained within the boundaries of the proportions. Even allowing for a few 'lost' balliboes or even the maps getting confused at times the 1609 survey is a good attempt at recording the basic requirements for a planning exercise. Without recourse to either maps or instruments and only listening to verbal descriptions it is unlikely that a stranger to a particular area of Ulster today would produce a map very different to those prepared in 1609.

JMC

Conditions of the Plantation

Although the commissioners had completed their survey by September 1609, the maps and report were not published for another five months. The new conditions incorporated most of the suggestions made by the Lord Deputy, and as the success of the Plantation was to be continuously assessed during the next twelve years the principal conditions must be kept in mind.

The confiscated land was divided into precincts or baronies which were subdivided into proportions. Large proportions were nominally 2,000 acres, middle proportions 1,500 acres, and small proportions 1,000 acres. Bog and woodland were added to the proportions free of rent. The principal undertaker in each precinct was given up to 3,000 acres; no other undertaker was to receive more than one great proportion. The grant was given in fee simple, with tenure in socage. The grant also allowed the undertaker to hold a manor court twice a year and also markets.

To assist in the success of the Plantation the undertakers were granted the right of duty-free importation from Great Britain for five years of the necessities of life not being used as merchandise. They could also export produce free of duty for up to seven years. They were entitled to cut timber required to build their homes, etc. from any woodlands for a period of two years, thereafter they could only cut timber on their own land.

The chief undertaker in a precinct was entitled to appoint the clergy of the parish. The undertakers had to pay rent at £5 6s. 8d. per 1,000 acres. They had to build within three years a strong bawn or courtyard plus, in the case of great proportions, a stone house, and on a middle proportion a stone or brick house. There had to be 10 families, giving 24 English or Irish Scots tenants of eighteen years or upwards, who were to be given land as follows:

2 freeholders of 120 acres
3 twenty-one-year leaseholders of 100 acres
4 cottagers or artificers

The tenants were to be encouraged to build houses in groups, not scattered, in a village. The tenants were to be armed and mustered twice a year by a government officer. One third had to be on their land by 1 November 1610, one third by the 1st May 1611 and the remainder by 1 November 1611. The undertakers had to take the Oath of Supremacy of the King over the Church. They had to be resident by mid-summer 1610 and were not to sell their land within five years without permission. They were not to let or sell land to the native Irish.

RJH, IW

Allocation of land in Strabane barony

Following the publication of the survey maps and conditions Strabane barony was divided into eleven proportions and allocated to eight undertakers. The barony was allocated to Scotsmen who had connections with the King. A description of the Plantation families is given later. Here we set down the timetable covering the allocation of land.

Three names were submitted to Dublin by 28 April 1610, probably nominated by the King. These were James Clapham, Sir John Drummond, and James Haig, who had their patents granted by the end of May or the beginning of June. James Hamilton, Earl of Abercorn, had been induced to become an undertaker by the King but he had complained that these three men had not been nominated by him. His patent was granted in August. However the remaining undertakers were all related to the Earl of Abercorn. Sir Claud Hamilton and Sir George Hamilton were his brothers, whilst Sir Thomas Boyd was his brother-in-law. George Hamilton was considered to be a relative, but his exact relationship with the Earl is not known. He had applied for land in 1609 and it could well be that he was a nominee of the King. They all received their grants at the end of August 1610.

The barony of Strabane was divided into 11 proportions and granted to eight undertakers as follows:

Proportion	Plantation Nominal Acreage	Plantation Statute Acreage	Actual Acreage	Undertaker
Strabane	1,000	1,625	13,450	James, 1st Earl of Abercorn
Dunalong	2,000	3,250	10,350	James, 1st Earl of Abercorn
Shean	1,500	2,450	12,650	Sir Thomas Boide (Boyd)
Largie or Cloghogenhall	1,500	2,450	12,400	Sir George Hamilton
Dirrywoon or Derrione	1,000	1,625	10,900	George Hamilton
Ballymagoieth or Ballenagneagh	1,000	1,625	10,050	Sir John Drummond
Newton	1,000	1,625	13,500	James Clapam (Clapham)
Lislapp	1,000	1,625	9,050	James Clapam (Clapham)
Tirenemuriertagh or Munterlony	1,500	2,450	24,900	James Haig(e)
Killenny	1,000	1,625	8,350	Sir Claud Hamilton
Eden or Teadane	1,000	1,625	9,650	Sir Claud Hamilton
Abbey Land			3,500	
Glebe Land			5,900	
Bishops Land			10,400	

Table showing allocation of lands in Strabane barony in 1610

As can be seen from the above table, the condition which laid down that the principal undertaker should receive two proportions and up to 3,000 acres and all others only one proportion was broken from the start as two undertakers James Clapham and Sir Claud Hamilton received two proportions. In addition the amount of land granted greatly exceeded the nominal acreage. The ownership of the land changed during the period, the dominant move being the rapid acquisition of land by the Hamilton family.

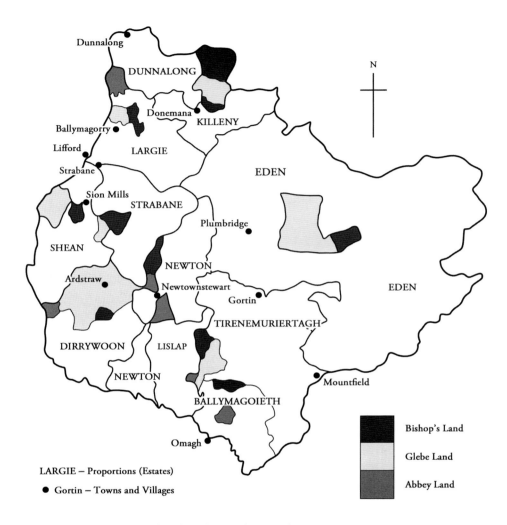

Map of Strabane barony showing Plantation proportions

Reference has been made to the inaccuracy of the surveys. This, together with the fact that some of the grants were not clearly written, resulted in disputes between undertakers. One example in the area arose out of a claim by Captain John Leigh, who had been granted the abbey of Omagh (Omey) and its associated land, that he was entitled to a number of balliboes in the Newtown proportion. These were Castle Moyle, Boltra, Cregaghie Dronteige Tullamucke and Strayinall. (The spelling of these balliboes is that given in the original document). In 1611 the Deputy Escheater found in favour of Leigh.

IW, JMC

The Plantation families

The allocation of land to the undertakers shows that the Hamiltons were the most prominent within the barony. James Hamilton, the 1st Earl of Abercorn, was the eldest son of Lord Claud Hamilton, 1st Baron Paisley. In 1598, at the age of twenty-three he became a privy councillor and gentleman of the bedchamber, at the Scottish Court. He received a charter to the lands of Abercorn (West Lothian) in 1601 and his earldom was conferred in 1606. When the possibility of a political union between England and Scotland was being considered in the years immediately following the union of the crowns, Abercorn acted as one of the Scottish commissioners during the negotiations. Abercorn did not volunteer to be responsible for the settlement of Strabane. From a letter written early in 1612, we learn that he was by 'induced' James to become an undertaker 'for a countenance and strength to the rest'. Nevertheless on 12 April 1610, the Earl wrote to the King to complain that he was not being permitted to exercise as much influence on arrangements for the Plantation in Strabane as he desired. He had received word, he explained, through Sir Alex Hay, the Scottish secretary, that there had been changes in Plantation plans, particularly concerning 'that litle yor matie apperit to think fitting for me Callit Strabawne (Strabane)'; as he understood, some of the proportions in Strabane were to be assigned to men not nominated by him. Without much doubt, the men to whom he referred were those on the list which had reached Dublin by the end of April.

The docquet for his own proportions of Strabane and Dunalong was granted in August 1610. In May 1611 the Lord Deputy was ordered to give the Earl 25 footmen from the army to aid his plantation and by November he and his wife had taken up residence within the barony. In the following February he was given the right to press any ship on the west coast of Scotland to supply him with transport to Ireland. By 1613 he had taken over Sir Thomas Boyd's neighbouring proportion of Shean. (The Earl had married Boyd's sister Marion.)

In 1615 he gave proof that he had fulfilled his undertaker's conditions and in August he received a payment of £30,000 (Scots), equivalent to £2,500 sterling, for services rendered. He surrendered the land and had it regranted on 18 October 1616. In 1617 his son, another James, was created Baron Strabane 'in consideration of his (Abercorn's) services in planting, a colony of brave men professing the true religion in the Strabane barony.' He died at Monckton in Scotland on 23 March 1618, some three years before his father, and was succeeded by his son James, who then became the 2nd Earl of Abercorn as well as the 1st Baron Strabane. The latter was then about fifteen years old and his uncle, Sir George Hamilton of Greenlaw, whose proportion was Largie or Cloghogenhall, was appointed his guardian.

Sir George Hamilton's docquet for his land was dated August 1610 and soon put in an appearance to develop his proportion. Perhaps the most striking feature about Sir George was his religion; he was a Roman Catholic. The earliest document to state this was dated 1614, but there is no reason to believe that he was converted after the Plantation had begun. Here, then, was the anomalous situation of a Roman Catholic being placed in charge of a segment of a plantation designed, in part, to establish a firm footing for Protestantism in Ireland. Perhaps even more significant that he also became the guardian of a second nephew, the heir of his brother Sir Claud Hamilton. He brought up both wards as Roman Catholics. Numerous Scottish Roman Catholics settled in Strabane barony which led the Bishop of Derry to warn (in 1630) that a rebellion would break out if such settlement was allowed to continue. However, he survived all the pressures and was the only one of the original undertakers to live throughout the period of this review.

Hamilton memorial in Paisley Abbey

Sir Claud Hamilton, the second son of Lord Claud Hamilton, was granted the proportions of Killeny and Eden. He married Janet Hamilton, heiress to Sir Robert Hamilton of Elistown. He became a privy councillor at the age of eighteen, and at was claimed by his son that he had served the crown. The only official post, apart from that of privy councillor, which he can be shown to have held, was deputy sheriff of Lanarkshire. However, Abercorn's letter to the king written in April 1610 mentioned a brother who, it was stated, would present his case at court. It is very probable that the brother in question was Sir Claud and that he was frequently close to the king. According to Sir Claud's son, Sir Claud became a planter on the initiative of the king and as a reward for services rendered. But the son was writing (about 1661) long after the patents were issued and was pleading a case at the time of writing. His testimony, therefore, must be treated cautiously. Given Sir Claud's close relationship to Abercorn, it seems likely that his brother was responsible for his grant though, no doubt, the King fully approved of it.

Sir Claud had purchased half of James Haig's proportion of Tirenemuriertagh in 1612. He showed little interest in his proportion. However, the King did make him an Irish privy councillor, but, four days after this appointment he died on 18 October 1614, having been in Ireland only a short time. In 1618, after his eldest son William came of age, Sir George Hamilton requested that Sir Claud's second son, Alexander, should inherit the Irish estates because William had inherited estates in Scotland as well as Ireland. Later this decision was reversed with a formal grant given to William in 1629.

Sir Thomas Boyd of Bedlay was granted the proportion of Shean in August 1610. He was the second son of the 6th Lord Boyd. His sister had married the 1st Earl of Abercorn which no doubt explains his selection as undertaker. Although he went to Ulster and had started building work, he had disposed of Shean to his brother-in-law by 1613, presumably to return to the family estates in Ayrshire.

Ruins of Derrywoon Castle, Barons Court

The last of the undertakers with a Hamilton connection was George Hamilton who received a patent for Derrywoon in August 1610 in return 'for good true and acceptable service'. He came from East Bynnie, Linlithgowshire (West Lothian) and was erroneously referred to as the Earl of Abercorn's brother in a grant of 1612. His precise relationship with the Earl has not been established. Although he took up residence in 1611, he had left by 1613 when Sir George Hamilton answered for him and who is recorded as the undertaker in 1618.

There were three undertakers who had been allocated land before the Earl of Abercorn. James Clapham had been a servant of the royal household in Scotland, but his origins are unknown. His patent to Newtown and Lislap was granted in May 1610 and he took possession in person in the following September, after having taken the oath of supremacy. He had divided the land between his four sons, but shortly afterwards (1615) had sold the estate to Sir Robert Newcomen for £1,400.

Sir John Drummond of Bordland came from Perthshire. He was granted Ballymagoieth in June 1610 and settled on the estate the following year. Although he built up the estate, it is reasonable to suppose that he spent some time each year in Scotland as he had been made a justice of the peace in Perthshire in 1613. He was succeeded by his brother Malcolm in May 1625 which was confirmed by a grant dated May 1629. However, by the end of the period of our survey this estate has passed to Sir William Stewart.

James Haig of Bemerside came from Berwickshire and having had some influence at the court had received a patent for Tirenemuriertagh in June 1610. However, he had to contend with disputes in Scotland and did not take up his proportion which was surrendered and regranted to Sir George Hamilton and Captain (later Sir) William Stewart in January 1613. Stewart had seen military service in Ulster since 1608 and as a Scottish servitor he had been granted land in the precinct of Kilmacrennan in County Donegal in 1610. He was knighted in 1613 and for two years represented County Donegal in the Irish Parliament. He had married Frances, the second daughter of Sir Robert Newcomen of Mosstoun, County Longford. Sir Robert was noted as the owner of this part of the proportion in the 1622 survey, but Sir William Stewart was regranted this part again in 1629. No doubt family arrangements were involved here.

It will be seen that Sir Robert Newcomen first came into the area in about 1615 and it was after this that Sir William Stewart became acquainted with him and his daughter. The latter had taken over his father-in-law's estates by 1630 and the Drummond estate by 1641. He was therefore the second largest landowner at the end of the period – Sir George Hamilton being the largest.

The last major landowner to appear was Sir Henry Tichborne. He was the fourth son of Sir Benjamin Tichborne of Hampshire and had been a captain of a foot regiment stationed in Ireland in 1620. Shortly afterwards he had become governor of Lifford, being knighted in 1623. He had probably become a sub-tenant of Sir George Hamilton in respect of some of the balliboes as well as part of the precinct of Loughmaguife in Clogher barony. He received a grant for the latter in 1629 and part of Tirenemuriertagh which was to be called the manor of Mountfull (Mountfield). He evidently continued in his military career for in 1641 he was residing at Finglass, County Dublin, whilst being governor of Drogheda.

MP-M, RJH, IW

Other Plantation people

It is possible to trace family histories of the principal landowners such as the Abercorns, down to the present time, and, it is noteworthy that the Abercorn family still reside in the Strabane area at Barons Court. It would be remarkable if we could trace Plantation families actually living today in the same balliboes (townlands) to which they moved from Scotland in the early seventeenth century. Only one example came to light during the study. John Hamilton of Priestfield had three sons, all of whom became the sub-tenants of undertakers: Robert 'whose successor enjoyeth a considerable estate called Caledon' (County Tyrone); Hugh; and William. The latter two obtained grants from the Earl of Abercorn for Loughneas and Lisdivin, and Ballyfatton respectively. A descendent of the last-named lived until recently in the same townland. William had been granted in 1617 freedom from the yoke of Scottish servitude and given all the rights and privileges of an English subject. A grant in 1634 from Lord Claud Hamilton confirmed his tenure of Ballyfatton at a rent of £18 per year. In the 1641 Rising he was taken prisoner by the rebels and taken to Doe Castle, County Donegal, where he and his nephew Robert suffered 'great privations' from which be died in 1642. He had married Janet Moore and they had nine children. However the Ballyfatton land had passed to his son John but was subsequently sold to his third son William whose descendents lived there until recently.

Early references to Scotsmen in the Strabane barony are to be found in the patents releasing them from Scottish servitude. These were mainly issued in 1616 and 1617. The list below shows where these Plantation immigrants settled and occasionally their trade.

Strabane: John Wallace snr; James Hatricke; James Gibbe; Thomas, John, David, John senior, John junior, and Thomas (carpenter) Stephenson; Thomas Cuthbertson, James Pooke, and James Hamilton (merchants), Andrew Arnett, David Morrison, William Kyle, John McIltyre, Mathew Corslaw, John Henderson (tailor), James Coope, Thomas Yonge; William Kennedy (carpenter) Alexander Craig; Peter Lawson; William Paterson; William Hamilton (merchants); James Sharpe (gent); Mathew Crafford and James Hamilton (servants to the Earl of Abercorn).

Pakusbanoke (Peacockbank): John Stephenson (Would he be a forebear of the Stephensons in the neighbouring Magheragar townland?)

Ballymagorry: Gilbert McCriaghane; Patrick & Archibald McCriaghane; John Montgomerie

Dunalong: John Doninge rufus; Gabriel Simpson; David and John Lyan; Rob Miller; Robert Granger

Urney: James Young (clerk)

Rateini (Ratyn): James Galbreth, senior and junior

Cariclsle (Carricklee): Robert Hamilton

Ballyfatton: William Hamilton

For the district around Strabane the next list of names to consider is the muster roll of 1630. This gives 208 names. For a complete list refer to *Ardstraw – Historical Survey of a Parish 1600–1900* by John H. Gebbie (1968). Only the following names given above appear in the 1630 list – James Gibbe (then provost of the corporation), William Hamilton, James Hatricke, William Patterson, John Wallace and Thomas Young. What happened to the other sixteen Strabane men released from Scottish servitude in 1616/7? One had apparently died around 1622 as discussed below. Was the muster roll a complete list of all immigrant men in 1630? This question is posed as a result of noting the names given in an 'indenture' referring to property in Strabane, dated 21 November 1627. Only the last two appear on the muster roll three years later: George Ferroll, Peter Lawson, William Barnes, James Duncan, Constantine Moretoune, Patrick Hamilton and William Ca(l)der.

Tombstone to Robert Granger (d. 1630), Grange Graveyard

For the Ballymagoieth, Newton and Lislap proportions, we can compare the certificated returns for the 1622 survey made by Sir John Drummond and Sir Robert Newcomen for their respective proportions, with the 1630 muster roll. In 1622 in Ballymagoieth we find listed two freeholders and 31 leaseholders, with some of the latter having Irish names. In the muster roll of 1630 Sir William Stewart gave 27 names for his lands in Strabane barony – he also had a 2,000 acre proportion in Clogher barony. Only one name is common to both lists. An inquisition referring to Drummond's 'tenants' in 1624 lists 23 names. Seven were the same as given in 1622, the remainder were mostly Irish.

Finally, early settlers are recorded in the indexes to wills. The dates given in the list below are for the granting of probate, giving an approximation for the date of the death of the person listed. For the period up to 1640 the following are noted in Strabane barony:

1617	John Moore, Strabane
1618	Lt. James Montgomerie, Ardstraw
1622	Thomas Stevenson, Cullydrummond, Urney parish (carpenter) (Is this the same Thomas Stevenson of Strabane referred to in the list of men who had obtained patents releasing them from Scottish servitude in 1616/7? Had he moved and set up a home at Cullydrummond some 4 miles from Strabane?)
1623	James Wetherspoon, Strabane (snapmaker) Archibald Campbell, Camus Francis Hogshead, Strabane
1629	John Mathers, Donagheady Patrick Gamble (Gemmill), Strabane John Love, Strabane
1631	Matthew Murdoch, Camus
1633	Patrick Stewart (gent), Pubble
1635	James Cawdor, Urney Andrew Haddowie, Strabane Rev. Patrick Hamilton, Donagheady. (He is not recorded as being a minister in any of the parishes in Strabane barony) Thomas Young, Strabane (Is he the same Thomas Yonge referred to in the list of men who had obtained patents releasing them from Scottish Servitude and in the muster roll?)
1636	Claud Wilson, Donagheady Alexander Harper, Ballymagorry Daniel McKey, Donagheady
1637	James Hamilton, Donagheady (Is he a relative of Hugh Hamilton claiming the tenancy of Lisdivin in 1640?)
1638	Archibald Young, Donagheady John Maine, Strabane
1639	George Halyburton, The Cortyn, Badoney parish
1640	Ellen Halyburth ale Waghup, The Cortyn, Badoney parish David Mitchell, Glencush

JMC

3
The Town of Strabane

General proposals for the establishment of towns

The Plantation of Ulster not only provided for the settlement of people on the land, it also proposed the establishment of a number of towns in each county as focal points. In the 'Project' of Plantation twenty-five corporate towns were envisaged. Some were to be new settlements or to be developed around the recently established forts in Ulster, others were to be at places of traditional Irish occupation. Land was to be granted to the corporations of these towns to provide for their development, and, to get them underway, it was suggested that there should be a 'leavy or presse' of tradesmen and artificers from England.

However, by the autumn of 1610 no townsmen had in fact been despatched from England, and the problem of town establishment remained unresolved. Apart altogether from their importance for the internal development of the colony, the proposed towns had a political role. Each would have the power to return two members to the Irish House of Commons, whose presence (it was assumed) would facilitate the passing of government legislation. In December 1610, after the land in the plantation counties had been allocated, the lord deputy in Dublin made proposals on the matter which proved acceptable in London. The effect of these was that an undertaker or servitor near to each proposed town should be appointed to superintend its development. The patron should introduce townsmen and ensure that houses were built. In return the land intended for the town should be granted to him.

It was on the basis of this decision, by and large, that the new towns were got under way. The result was that when they were incorporated, they did not

receive corporate grants of the town land, and so their income from the start
was severely limited. By 1613 fourteen places in the six escheated counties
had received charters, increasing later to sixteen.

RJH

Strabane before the Plantation

Strabane immediately before the Plantation would have been an unimpressive
place. In 1598 County Tyrone was described as having no towns 'but divers
ruined Castles' of which Strabane was listed as one. The appropriate maps of
the escheated counties depict it as small in comparison with Lifford. The
evidence of a contemporary corroborates this impression. Thomas
Blenerhasset, a grantee in Fermanagh, published in 1610 a pamphlet
resulting from an Ulster visit. He described the present decay of Armagh in
pungent phrases; indeed it was a 'base and abject thing not much better than
Strabane'.

There had been Scottish settlement in the area prior to the Plantation.
Turlough Luineach O'Neill had married Lady Agnes Campbell in 1569, who
brought with her a thousand Scots mercenaries. This number was increased
from time to time. In 1598 it was recorded that there were 'above 3 or four
score Scottish families inhabitting' at Strabane. How these were affected by
Docwra's campaign and Sir Art Og's submission in the closing years of the
O'Neill was cannot be established. In 1608 the Scottish settlement at
Strabane fled to Lifford during Sir Cahir O'Dogherty's rebellion. This
group would have links with the much better documented pre-Plantation
colony at Docwra's Derry which, though largely English, contained a small
component of

Extract from map of *c.* 1601 showing
Strabane and Lifford

Lowland Scots. Opportunity for them at Strabane would have arisen from the political attitude of Turlough O'Neill, son of Sir Art Og, and their presence there may have been promoted, in part at least, by George Montgomery, a Scot who had recently been appointed Protestant bishop of Derry, Raphoe and Clogher. It may have been to these people that lord deputy Chichester was referring in October 1608, when the formal plantation was being planned, when he said that 'divers Scottishmen' were willing to plant at Strabane 'and make it a pretty town'. The introduction of the Plantation, however, in 1610 radically altered the situation. Strabane and adjacent lands was now allocated as part of the barony of Strabane to Scottish undertakers and Turlough O'Neill and his brothers were displaced to Dungannon barony. It can be assumed that many (if not all) of these early Scots settlers stayed on under Abercorn.

RJH

The growth of Strabane

Strabane, although previously an important old Irish position, was not one of the five places in Tyrone designated for incorporation and allocated land in the 'Project' of Plantation in *c.* January 1609. The explanation may perhaps be found is that no final decision had then been taken about the custodian grant of land in this area made earlier to the sons of Sir Art Og O'Neill (Turlough Luineach's son), or in the fact that it was proposed to establish a town at Lifford, a fortified centre, immediately nearby. Whatever caused the change in decision – perhaps the energy and status of Abercorn – the incorporation of Strabane in 1613 made it a corporation for which no landed endowment had originally been designated, and brought its patron, Abercorn, no land beyond and above that of his proportion in which it was located.

The government surveys of the development of the Plantation are ambiguous in that it is not easy to distinguish between developments in the town and on the estates of the undertakers. By 1611, Carew reported, Abercorn had built some large timber houses and a brewhouse neere the towne of Straban' surrounded by a court and his tenants had built sixty houses. Bodley, in 1613, described a similar situation. He describes Abercorn's

Representation of Strabane on Down Survey map of *c.* 1655

building as a 'large thatched house ... at Strabane'. Both indicate that the landlord's house was intended to be temporary. It would seem likely that Abercorn's activity 'neere the towns of Straban' indicates 'that he had chosen a new site, near to the present town centre, some distance from the old O'Neill headquarters. Many of the tenants' houses referred to must have been nearby, thus forming the nucleus of the settlement. By the time of its incorporation in 1613 Strabane was still small.

Pynnar's survey of 1618–19 indicates the dimensions of intervening developments. Abercorn had built on his Strabane proportion a 'strong and fair' castle (but no bawn) and a school house of lime and stone. The building of a church, the walls whereof were about five feet high had been 'at a stay ever since the late earl died' (23 March 1618). The town built 'about this castle' is described as

> consisting of 80 houses, whereof many of them are of lime and stone, very well and strongly built;

and the report continues somewhat ambiguously

> there are many other good timber houses; in these houses there are 120 families who are able to make 200 men, every one having arms for his defence.

However, the total number of British tenants Pynnar recorded as 'planted and estated' on the entire proportion of Strabane was 65 families consisting of

William Hamilton memorial in Camus-juxta-Mourne Parish Church, Strabane

180 men – merchants and tradesmen and some 'cottagers' including 53 townsmen each having a house, a garden plot, and 'some small quantities of land'. Even accepting the figure of 53 townsmen which might imply close on 100 adult males, Strabane was now larger than most of the other towns, except Derry, in the six escheated counties.

Pynnar's reference to merchants can be amplified from other sources. The advantageous position of the town on the Foyle gave it potential as an outport of Derry. The ship, the *Gift of God* of Strabane, burden twenty tons and masters Mathew and Robert Lindsay, is seen to be engaged in trading with Scotland in the port book of Derry for 1614–15. (See pages 66–7.) In addition, names of six of the first corporators of Strabane, John Kennedie, James Kile, John Browne, William Hamilton, Hugh Hamilton and John Brisbane (or Bersban) also appear as merchants paying customs duties at Derry. Some of them received grants of denization in 1616, and these lists include in addition 'John Stephenson junr., Thomas Cuthbertson, James Pooke and James Hamilton of Strabane, merchants'. Strabane was thus fulfilling the trading needs of the Scottish colony of which it was the urban focus. The few surviving records of this trade show it to have been with Renfrew in Scotland, near to the home district of the Earl of Abercorn,

A detailed picture of the state of the town emerges at the time of the inquiry into the Plantation by commissioners in 1622. It contained a 'strong' castle of stone and lime, and 'above' 100 dwelling houses 'diverse of them of stone and lyme' and 120 British families, comprising 200 able men armed with shot and pike. The number of houses is greater than Pynnar's figure, the number of people identical. There was also a 'sessions house, and a market cross of stone and lime with a strong roome under it to keep prisoners in and a Plattforme on the top w'ch is a place of good defence', Such buildings were unusual outside county towns in Ulster, and indeed had not been completed there in all cases by this time. In addition there was a watermill stone-built 'with a bridge over the waters w'ch runneth by the said mill' erected at the expense of the former Earl. The commissioners further stated that thirty of the inhabitants were free each having a house, a garden, and 'smale quantities of land'. The commissioners' report was based on their own inquiries as well as on the scrutinisation of certificates presented to them by the undertakers. The report on the Abercorn estate was presented by the agent, William Lynn, an energetic figure who had migrated about 1606 from the infant Scottish settlements in County Down to the pre-Plantation settlement at Derry. It indicates that the 'strong rooms' under the market cross was merely a place of temporary detention for prisoners prior to their removal to the king's jail at Dungannon. Lynn added further that there existed a boat for men and horses at Strabane upon the River Mourne 'for passage upon any inundac'on or swelling of that river'.

Further evidence of the substantial size of the town is given in the muster roll of 1630. The entry of the 'men and armes of the town, lists 208, who between them mustered arms as follows: 140 swords, 53 snaphances, 45 or 46 pikes, 10 callivers, 4 muskets and 2 halberts. In addition, five had bandoleers and there was a bearer of the colours. Sixty-three of those who mustered showed no arms at all. On this showing, the Strabane townsmen were not heavily armed. The list is probably not entirely exhaustive as a census of adult males, but materials to criticise it by are scant and few. (For a complete list of names refer to *Ardstraw – Historical Survey of a Parish* by John H. Gebbie (1968)). However, an indenture of 20 October 1627 between the landlord and a Strabane freeholder, provides five settler names, probably also townsmen, which do not appear on the muster roll. These are George Ferroll, Peter Lawson, William Barnes, James Duncan and Constantine Moretoune.

We can assume a total settler population of some 500 people – men, women and children. How many Irish lived in the town is not known, if in fact any had lived there – the small pre-Plantation settlement could well have been settled only by the Scots referred to earlier. Not many towns in the six planted counties exceeded fifty British adult males, though Armagh had about one hundred. With the exception of the striking development of Derry and Coleraine on the Londoners' Plantation, which had 500 and 300 adult males respectively at this time, Strabane was substantially larger than its counterparts in the escheated counties. At the same time it had not grown significantly since 1622. There is no similar material for the study of the town's population in the next decade.

A very wide spectrum of Scottish names is represented amongst the townsmen recorded on the muster roll. Names occurring five time or over were Cunningham (8), Hamilton (5), Home, Homes or Humes (6), Paterson (5), Robertson and Robinson (5), Smyth or Smith (6), and Wallace (5). A noteworthy feature is that 22, or some 10%, had Mac– names, for example MacFarlan, MacNeil, and MacMichael. The townsmen were doubtless predominantly Lowland Scots as the plan of Plantation required. Many of those with Highland names probably came, however, from the Abercorn homeland in Renfrewshire in the northwest Lowlands, or were descendants of the 16th-century mercenaries.

RJH

The members of the first corporation

In 1611 the incorporation of Strabane was decided on, and it received its charter in 1613 in common with most of the other incorporated towns in the plantation. A warrant for incorporation was issued by the lord deputy on 25 November 1612, and the charter followed on 18 March 1613. An analysis of the composition of the corporation, which is common with the majority of the town corporations of this time, was made up of thirteen designated members.

Biographical sketches of the original provost and first twelve burgesses follow:

Patrick Crawford

Patrick Crawford, the first provost or mayor, was one of two Scottish captains sent with soldiers to help suppress O'Dogherty's rising in 1608. He was stationed at Lifford. In the following years he continued at Lifford, though he may have been at Strabane for a time. He was selected as a servitor grantee in the Plantation in Donegal and in September 1611, as Patrick Crawford of Lifford, he received a grant of lands at Letterkenny. Furthermore, he retained military connections and was killed on a naval expedition to suppress a rising on the Scottish island of Islay in 1614. In November 1615 royal instructions for the granting of his lands at Letterkenny to his widow's new husband referred to him as formerly of Lifford. It is clear that at the time of his appointment as first officer of Strabane he was a prestigious figure, not resident in the town but prominent locally. He was Scottish but a Donegal servitor and held the position which in a number of the other Ulster corporations would have been taken by the landlord himself.

Hugh Hamilton

Three were Hamiltons, confusingly two Williams and a Hugh, though none of them of the immediate family circle of the Earl. All three developed careers with a considerable rural basis. Hugh Hamilton, the third son of John Hamilton of Priestfield in Blantyre, Lanarkshire, in 1603, had been apprenticed in Edinburgh. In Ulster he combined his mercantile pursuits with the acquisition of leasehold land. In 1616 he received a grant of denization as of Loghneneas, merchant, and by 1622 he was a freeholder of two townlands, modern Cloghcor and Loughneas, on the estate of Largie or Cloghogenall, granted to Sir George Hamilton of Greenlaw, brother of the earl of Abercorn. He was also a freeholder of modern Lisdivin Lower and Upper on the Earl of Abercorn's Dunalong estate, having received this land from the Earl of Abercorn on 1 January 1615. He had built a stone house by 1622. By the time of his death in 1637 he had acquired interests in the abbey or grange land of Burndennet with its tithes and fishing. He bequeathed these lands as well as 'houses in Strabane' in his will. One of his executors was his brother-in-law, James Gibb of Strabane, who had been provost of the town in 1630. He was himself provost of Strabane in 1625.

William Hamilton (1)

William Hamilton of Strabane, merchant, who received a fee-farm grant from the Earl of Abercorn of a messuage or tenement and a garden plot with two acres of land nearby on 1 March 1616, was probably the same person as that William Hamilton who features in the Derry port book of 1614–15 as a merchant, and who had received a grant of denization on 17 August 1616. By 1622 he was a freeholder of one townland on the Earl of Abercorn's Strabane estate and on which he had built a stone house.

William Hamilton (2)

The other William Hamilton was a more substantial person. He was of Wedderhill in Fife, born about 1577, and a grandson of John Hamilton, archbishop of St Andrews. He married in Scotland in 1613. He received a grant of denization in 1616 as of Trien-Itragh, part of the Earl of Abercorn's Strabane estate, and it emerges that by 1622 that he was a freeholder of four townlands and had built a stone house. However he quickly seems to have decided to expand his interests into the less competitively settled English undertakers' barony of Omagh. In 1622 it was stated that William Hamilton, 'now Provost of Strabane' did usually dwell in the castle on the Fentonagh (not modern Fintona) estate then owned by Sir Henry Mervyn, though Hamilton was 'not there now but comes tither again at Michaelmas next'. From 1625 he most commonly appears as of Loughmuck, also Mervyn land, though in 1636 he (or a namesake) appears as of Tirmegan, the freehold land he held from the Earl of Abercorn, and which in 1638 he mortgaged to William Hamilton of Ballyfatton, a prominent namesake, elder brother of Hugh Hamilton, whose family was probably connected to the Hamiltons of Binning (represented in Strabane barony by the undertaker George Hamilton), and whose son William his daughter Isabel had married in 1630. Thus while it is stated that he also had a house in Strabane there is no reason to believe that he lived there for any substantial period. In the 1630 muster roll he is listed as holding 1,000 acres of churchlands as well, with a colony of fourteen British males beneath him. Not surprisingly he played a prominent part in county administration. He was a justice of the peace in 1622 as well as being provost of the town. Quarter sessions were held before him as of the justices of the peace at Strabane on 20 July 1630 when he was again provost, and he appears as a justice of the peace again in 1632, 1633, 1634 and 1635. In 1625 he had been high sheriff of the county, and held this office again in 1638. He died in 1668.

John Wilson and James Kile

Two of the first burgesses, John Wilson and James Kile, were present as jurors at the taking of an inquisition at Strabane as early as November 1611. Kile appears as a merchant in the Derry port book of 1614–15. His subsequent fortunes are obscure, but John Kiell, a possible relative, appears as a resident in the town in 1630. John Wilson of Strabane was a juror at the Tyrone assizes held at Dungannon in August 1615. He remained in Strabane, making his will there in December 1620 in which he left his property and modest legacies to his wife and family and desired to be buried in the parish church of Leckpatrick. A Robert Wilson who is listed amongst those who mustered for the town in 1630 could well have been his eldest son and William Wilson and John Wilson who are also listed were probably his other sons.

James Montgomery

James Montgomery is of special interest because his connexion with the town probably did not derive from the colonising efforts of the Earl of Abercorn. He is likely to be that James Montgomery who held a lease of the churchlands of Ardstraw and so would probably have been connected with George Montgomery, bishop of Derry, Raphoe and Clogher from 1605. Since the bishop surrendered Derry and Raphoe, though not Clogher, on his appointment to Meath, on 4 August 1610, James Montgomery's connexions with the area would have dated from just before the Plantation. He was thus a Scot, but with ecclesiastical rather than lay undertaker origins. He cannot have had any long-term association with the town, however, because his address when he received a grant of denization in 1616 was Tullonefert (modern Tullanavert), a townland amongst the episcopal lands near Clogher which were in the hands of the Montgomery family. There is no Montgomery on the muster roll for the town.

John Browne

If John Browne, another of the twelve first burgesses, be that John Browne who on 27 September 1607 received a patent to establish ferries in Donegal including one between Lifford and Strabane, then he provides a second link with earlier British activity in the northwest. A John Browne also occurs as a merchant in the Derry port books. Browne appears to have developed his connexions with the town. He was witness to a will there in 1620, provost and a justice of peace in 1628, and again in 1634. A John Browne wrote a letter from Strabane in July 1634 to the bishop of Derry on behalf of 'the inhabitants of Strabane' concerning church buildings. John Browne occurs on the muster roll of the town in 1630.

James Colville and John Birsbean

James Colville, another incorporator, lived at Strabane in March 1614 when his name survives as a juror, but by 1622 he was a freeholder on the Earl of Abercorn's Strabane estate and had built a house. John Birsbean (or Brisbaine), a burgess who also appears as a merchant in the Derry port books of 1614–15, is yet another who became a freeholder under the Earl of Abercorn. He sold his freehold to his brother William, and may well have been dead by 1622 or shortly thereafter. John's name disappears, whereas William is recorded as of Ardstraw (the parish in which the freehold was located) in 1625. He was high sheriff of the county in 1628. In 1636 he was provost of Strabane and quarter sessions were held before him and other justices of the peace there in July of that year. A William Birsben on the town muster roll in 1630 was probably a relative.

Thomas McAlexander, David Moncreefe and John Kennedy

Thomas McAlexander appears to have continued to reside in the town. He was provost of Strabane in 1618, and again in 1626 and 1633. A Thomas Alexander mustered in 1630. The same applies to David Moncreefe. He is mentioned as David Moncrieff of Strabane in 1625 and again in 1628. Two David Montcrieffs mustered for the town in 1630. John Kennedy, the last burgess, is also found trading through the port of Derry in 1614–15, and is recorded simply as a leaseholder on the Earl of Abercorn's Dunalong estate in 1622.

Many of the first burgesses, then, were directly involved, at least initially, in the affairs of the inceptive town, though most developed landed interests in the county while at the same time continuing to play some role in the government of the town. While perhaps only James Montgomery severed his connection with Strabane, only a few of the burgesses appear to have lived in it continuously. The number who were merchants is noteworthy as is also those who became freeholders of land. Doubtless a few, like Hugh Hamilton and William Hamilton of Loughmuck, and Patrick Crawford the first provost, owed their selection to their origins and substance, rather than to their intentions to reside in the town and supervise its development. The careers of all these men as outlined above, shows the connections between town and countryside and of their own developing fortunes in Plantation Ulster.

RJH

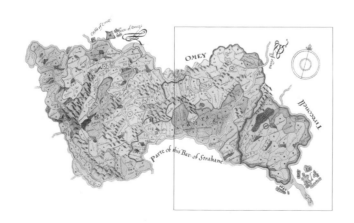

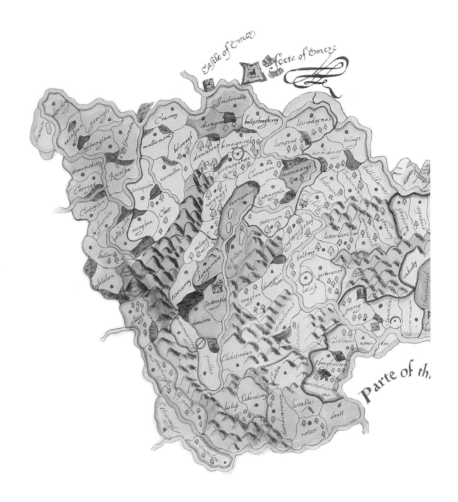

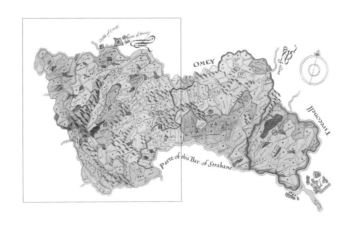

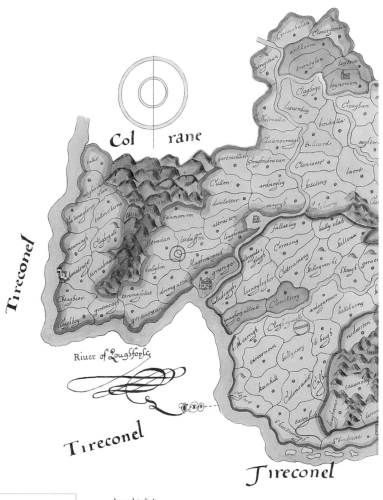

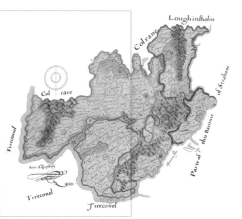

As part of the preparations for the Plantation, in 1609 maps were prepared of the escheated counties under the direction of Sir Josias Bodley. These were arranged by barony and two maps were prepared for the barony of Strabane. See pages 11–13 of this book for the background to these maps

The Strabane charter

The charter of Strabane is similar to those of the other Ulster and Irish towns incorporated at that time. It stated that the town area should be 'one entire and free borough,' within which there should be a 'body corporate and politic' consisting of a provost, twelve free burgesses and the commons with the power of perpetual succession and legal rights. The provost and burgesses were empowered to elect and return two members to each parliament. The first provost and burgesses were nominated in the charter 'to the intent that it may appear in future times that this new incorporation is composed of worthy and honest men'. These were to hold office, in the case of the first provost until the ensuing Michaelmas, and in the cases of the burgesses during life unless removed under exceptional circumstances. All the inhabitants of the town and such as the provost and burgesses might at any time admit to the freedom of the town were constituted to commons.

The provost should take the oath of supremacy before the justices of assize at the next general sessions for the county, as well as an oath to fulfil his duties of office. The provost should be elected annually by the burgesses, who should meet together on the feast of St John the Baptist in a suitable place within the town. He should hold office from the ensuing Michaelmas for one year, but before he be admitted he should take the oath of supremacy and his oath of office in the presence of the preceding chief officer. Should he die or in any manner vacate the office during his term a successor might be elected from amongst the burgesses to complete the term. On all occasions when a vacancy should occur amongst the burgesses, either by death or removal from office, the others might assemble and elect 'one or as many more as are deficient … from the better or more worthy inhabitants of the borough' to take the vacant place. The corporation might hold a weekly court of record, to be held before the provost, every Monday, to hear civil actions not exceeding the sum of five marks. The provost, burgesses and commons might assemble from time to time to make bye-laws and impose penalties for the breach of them, provided that these were reasonable and not repugnant to statute. The corporation might appoint two sergeants-at-mace and other necessary municipal officers. The corporation might hold a weekly market every Tuesday and two fairs annually, on 1 November and 1 May, the provost to be clerk of the market.

The essential feature of the charter is that civic government was vested in a small self-electing group. That the provost must take the oath of supremacy may be noted. The composition of the first nominated government was entirely settled. It is probably significant of the scale of development

Extract from patent of Newton and Lislap to James Clapham, 1610 (PRONI)

envisaged in the town at the time of incorporation that no provision was made in the charter for the organisation of specialist craft guilds. One of the most notable features of the charter is that it did not contain a grant of the town site or any land. Strabane had not been amongst those places originally intended for incorporation, and so no land had been earmarked in 1609 as an endowment for the town. The corporate income was thus of necessity severely limited. The financial returns from courts and fairs and markets would not have been great.

RJH

The corporation of Strabane

In 1622 the corporation of the town presented a petition to the commissioners then conducting an inquiry into the progress of the Plantation in general. They pointed out that although the borough was 'scituated in an eminent place, incorporated and peopled with a good number of inhabitants', because 'they have not one foote of land given or belonging to the … towne', they could not perform the King's service 'either in buying and maintayneing of armes, bearing of two burgesses expences at every parliament, paying of subsidies and taxations and fulfilling such offices and duties as of the like place are expected.' They suggested that some additional land should be granted to the heirs of the Earl of Abercorn, so that they, in exchange, could hand over a corresponding area of land to the corporation. This might just have been possible in 1622 because owing to omissions in the maps of 1609 there were still small areas of land throughout the Plantation which had not yet been granted out to proprietors – concealed lands as they were called. However, no action was in fact taken to benefit the Strabane corporation, although the commissioners in their report added their weight to the petition.

Because corporation records for the period do not survive no detailed assessment of the role of the corporation can be made. The following is all that can be assembled of the succession of provosts prior to 1641 – Patrick Crawford, 1613; Thomas McAlexander, 1617–18; William Hamilton, 1621–22; Hugh Hamilton, 1624–25; Thomas McAlexander, 1626–27; John Browne, 1627–28 James Gibb, 1629–30; William Hamilton, 1630–31; Thomas McAlexander, 1632–33; John Browne, 1633–34; [William] Brisbane, 1635–36. It can be seen that the members of the first nominated corporation continued to hold the chief office and rotate it amongst themselves more or less throughout our entire period. Only two of the above people, James Gibb and [William] Brisbane, do not appear in the charter, but James Gibb was brother-in-law of Hugh Hamilton and [William] Brisbane had taken the place of his brother. The corporation was clearly a closely-knit body. How effective it was and how often it met is not clear. It is unlikely that any significant salary for the chief officer could have been raised. Yet although the provost in 1622, William Hamilton, had landed interests away from the town, the corporation was energetic enough to put in the petition just discussed. John Browne, in 1634, communicated with the bishop of Derry on church problems, at a time when ecclesiastical matters were under review. They could at least rise to the occasion. That the provost was regarded at the time as a person with an important supervisory function appears on two occasions, in 1629 and 1640, when the bishop sought action by him and consulted with him on matters of religious unorthodoxy in the town. In 1629 it was apparent to the bishop that the provost was in awe of the landlord, and he wrote ordering him not to obstruct the provost. In the last resort the initiative of the corporation would depend on the goodwill of the landlord.

RJH

The town and its landlord

At least under the 1st Earl relations of townsmen and landlord appear to have been very harmonious. Both Pynnar and the 1622 commissioners state that freeholders had been created in the town, but give conflicting statements of their numbers. The commissioners' report had adopted the agent's figure. Lynn referred to 'aboute the number of thirty persons who have a freeholde within the Burgh of Straban of a house and a garden and many of acres of land'. It seems clear that these, or most of these houses had been built by the Earl of Abercorn. An indenture, amongst the Abercorn papers, may be taken to illustrate the conditions of these freeholders. On 1 March 1616 William Hamilton of Strabane, merchant (one of the burgesses) received a fee-farm grant from the earl of a 'messuage or tenement and garden plotte' in the town, 64 feet wide and 150 feet long and also two acres in the 'holme', of Strabane. He might cut turf in any of the earl's 'mosses … to dispend in and upon the premises and not elsewhere.' In return Hamilton should pay an annual rent of £1 sterling, and also six hens, two capons and two days work with a man and a horse. He should do suit of court to the courts of the manor and perform all bye-laws and orders there enacted. He should also do suit of mill to the Earl's mill. It would seem, then, that Abercorn had built at least some of the houses in the town rather than granting building leases, a device which transferred that responsibility to the tenant. If this is correct, it must have been an important factor in the growth of the town.

The 1st Earl was not the only landlord in this period to create freeholders in the town. A fee-farm grant of 20 October 1627 made by Claud Hamilton to George Ferroll of Strabane was similar to the earlier indenture outlined above. Ferroll received a holding in Strabane and a 'small parcel of ground or garden plott' on the east side of the town. The annual rent and other conditions were identical to those of William Hamilton in 1616. The Civil Survey (1654–56) description of the town, as of 1641, would thus appear to be well-founded. Referring to two and one-third ballyboes (or townlands) 'whereon the corporac'on Towne of Strabane is sett', it states that this land is 'lett in tenements and acres to ye inhabitants of the Corporac'on to most of them in fee farme.'

While it is clear that an Irish population survived on the Abercorn estates, what evidence we have does not indicate any noteworthy, or indeed any, Irish presence within the town. The implications of this – the obligation for Irish formerly there to move – are not easy to quantify, but the impression is that the Irish population at Strabane on the eve of plantation was quite small. We know that three of the sons of Sir Art Og O'Neill (grandsons of Turlough Luineach) received grants of land in Dungannon barony under the Plantation, and that some of Turlough's followers removed with him. Thus the new and much larger settlement, overridingly colonist in composition, represented a break with the past.

With no contemporary map surviving to guide us, we can say little about the topography and layout of the town in this period. Tradition has it that the O'Neill castle was on the site of the former Flax Market in Barrack Street and that the Abercorn castle was located next to the site of the former Abercorn Hotel in Castle Street. This suggests a minor change in position at the time of Plantation. Whatever the shape of the town, it would seem that many of the houses had largish garden plots. No doubt some inns and wine-taverns could be found, but references to shops or shambles have not been discovered. Public buildings – the church, the sessions house and school – gave it an elementary dignity, but the dominating structure must have been the Abercorn castle, which was expanded in the 1630s. Being ungarrisoned, Strabane was without any major fortification. It was unwalled. Will inventories to describe the houses and their contents, wills themselves to indicate the wealth of individuals, and taxation records to throw light on social groupings are all missing from amongst the source materials.

It has, however, already been possible to indicate the occupations of many of the more substantial residents. At some time clergy of both denominations lived there. Beyond this we have only fleeting references to occupations. In 1622 it was noted that some of the tenants of land in Sir George Hamilton's estate lived at Strabane. The names of two carpenters (Thomas Stephenson and William Kennedy) and a tailor (John Henderson) living in Strabane occur in a list of those given a grant of denization in 1616. Undoubtedly many essential crafts were represented, but it is also likely that many residents were unskilled labourers and cottagers. Some must have been engaged in the salmon fishing on the River Mourne. We know nothing of the functioning of the guild merchant provided by charter. Much of the importance of the town derived from its fairs and markets whereby it provided essential facilities to the surrounding countryside. In a protest about the burden of soldiers stationed at Derry, the mayor and other officers of Derry, in April 1641, suggested that the load might be shared by Strabane:

> Strabane hath no souldiers, it is a populous towne and the best markett in this country, and but tenn myles hence, upon the same river.

This albeit loaded statement is our only comment on the town on the eve of 1641. The commissioners in 1622 had recognised its special potential.

> This plantation being cherished by your Majesties favour is like to prosper, and to grows unto a good strength for the defence of those panes; for we find that the inhabitants are very industrious; and doe daylie beautifie their towne with new buildings, strong and defencible …

Although Strabane could have little urban sophistication, nevertheless by 1641 the energetic Hamilton landlords had brought into existence a town considerably larger than most of its kind in Plantation Ulster. Favourable geographical location must have encouraged a combination of merchants, traders and farming people well suited to promote a single form of economic development.

RJH

4

The churches
and religious influence

Background

Churches had been established in the Strabane barony as long ago as the 5th Century, the earliest and most important historically being Ardstraw. It is reputed that St Patrick ordained Bishop MacErcae there. St Eugene, Bishop of Cenel Eogain had his church at Ardstraw. He died about 550. Ardstraw was briefly a diocese in its own right in the 12th century. Prior to the Plantation the last notable event was the burial of Turlough Luineach O'Neill in 1595 following his death in Strabane.

Early references to other churches in the area include one for Donagheady in the 7th century. Names of abbots at Camus are recorded in the 6th and 7th centuries. Monasteries for both women and (later) men were established at an early date at Urney. By the end of the 16th century the parishes in the Strabane Barony were Ardstraw, Badoney, Camus-juxta-Mourne, Cappy (or Cappagh), Donagheady, Leckpatrick and Urney. There had also been three Franciscan monastic settlements in Strabane barony – at Pubble, Corrick and Scarvagherin (Garvagh Keerin). In 1604 the latter comprised the site of the friary, a ruinous church with churchyard and half a quarter of land. Both Scarvagherin and Corrick had been granted to Robert Leicester in 1604 who in turn transferred his interest to Captain Daniel Leigh who had been granted abbey and other land at Omagh (Omey). In 1613 the King confirmed that Daniel and John Leigh be granted the land of these three monastic sites which had been allocated to undertakers in error. None of the documents consulted make any reference to a monastic site or building at Strabane.

Mrs McG, JMC

The bishops

The parishes in Strabane barony formed part of the diocese of Derry. In 1605 James I appointed a Scot, George Montgomery, as bishop of Derry, Raphoe and Clogher, thereby giving him a unique position in the northwest of Ireland. He received his grant to the bishoprics on 13 June 1605 but did not cross to Ireland to reside in Derry until the autumn of the following year. During this period he began to examine what lands the Church might claim. At the same time hand-picked clergy were being chosen for the job of converting the Irish to Protestantism.

After his arrival in Ireland Montgomery travelled throughout his dioceses and strengthened the financial position of his clergy. From 1607 to 1610 he granted leases to people who had been persuaded to come to the northwest of Ireland from the west and southwest of Scotland. Some of these may have settled in Strabane barony with its extensive churchlands. On 1 August 1610 he formally surrendered to the King the dioceses' possessions. Two days later Montgomery was given a new grant which listed all the lands to be administered by the Church. The next day he resigned from the dioceses of Derry and Raphoe, retained Clogher and was translated to the diocese of Meath as a reward for good service in Derry and Raphoe. The people who were settled by Montgomery have left few traces behind them. However, more is known of Montgomery's role in events leading up to the Flight of the Earls in September 1607.

The Bishop posed the greatest threat to the Earl of Tyrone as a result of the former's attempt to increase the land to be administered by the Church. It is clear that the Church claimed far more land than it could prove it owned, and, that if all land claimed was confirmed as belonging to the Church the Earl's position would have been greatly weakened. The Earl had also fallen out with one of his vassals, Sir Donnell O'Cahan and here also the Bishop aggravated the situation when

Bishop George Montgomery

he was summoned to London for an adjudication on the quarrel by the King. The Earl took fright, believing himself likely to be imprisoned, fled the country with the Earl of Tyrconnell and Cuconnaught Maguire of Fermanagh.

Brutus Babington was appointed bishop of Derry on 11 August 1610 and on 9 November was given formal possession of the land and property of the See of Derry. Babington died the following September. During his short term of office he was successful in persuading many Catholic clergy to conform to the uses and liturgy of the Church of Ireland. On 21 December 1611, Christopher Hampton was appointed Bishop.

Shortly before this on 4 November an inquisition had been held at Strabane at which jurors in the area embraced by the see of Derry had pointed out that glebe land had been given to Montgomery and requested that it should revert to the possession of the incumbent of a particular parish. This was rectified in the grant of 25 May 1615 to John Tanner who had succeeded Hampton on 13 May 1613. John Tanner died in 1615 and was succeeded by George Downham on 6 September 1616. He formally surrendered the possessions of the see on 17 December 1616 and had them regranted on 12 February 1617. Downham remained bishop until 1634 when John Bramhall, who was Wentworth's (appointed lord deputy of Ireland in 1633) close adviser, took over. These two men invoked a stronger adherence of the Church of Ireland to the ways of the Church of England. In the convocation of 1634–5 it was decreed that the Church of Ireland should follow the 39 Articles of the Church of England which meant that the 104 Articles agreed on in 1615 by the Church of Ireland, which had given a Calvinist slant to the Church's doctrines, were abandoned. As many of the ministers at that time had been either more Roman Catholic or Presbyterian inclined they were excommunicated, deposed or left their parishes. This explains the appearance of new ministers in the parishes after 1634.

JMC, IW

Landlords and laity

The Protestantism of the 1st Earl of Abercorn does not seem to be in question, although his widow, Marion Boyd, was charged with being a Roman Catholic by the Presbytery of Paisley in 1628. His energy and orthodoxy were taken note of in 1617 when he was commended for 'planting a colony of brave men, professing the true religion'. But both his elder son James who succeeded to the title, and his second son Claud who succeeded to the Strabane estate, who were minors when their father died, were Catholics. Sir George Hamilton of Greenlaw, their uncle, who eventually controlled five of the proportions in Strabane barony, was recognised as a Catholic as early as 1614, and described as 'an archpapist and a great patron of them' in 1622.

It was not, however, until 1629 when Anglo-Spanish war had exacerbated relations within Ireland that the issue of Catholicism amongst the settlers within Strabane barony came to the fore. As well as that, both Claud, the Master of Abercorn, who would in due course inherit the Strabane lands, and Sir William, who had taken over the estate of his father Sir Claud Hamilton of Shawfield, were Catholics. In these circumstances, local, national and international, it is not surprising that the bishop of Derry, George Downham, intervened. A number of points emerge from the surviving documents, which were sent to the Dublin government by the bishop.

The bishop's case was that not only were the Hamilton landlords active Catholics, but that also a number of Catholic clergy were harboured in the barony, including in particular Dr Owen McSweeney, vicar apostolic, or 'titular bishop', of the diocese of Derry and on his departure having been appointed to Kilmore, his successor Turlough O'Kelly, 'a more dangerous fellow' because of his alleged contacts with the Irish regiment in the Spanish Netherlands; and, also Thomas Blackney, a Jesuit. These were, in the bishop's words, 'doing much harm in the barony and town of Strabane'. Downham stated that in an interview with Claud, the Master of Abercorn, he had urged him 'if he would not embrace the reformed religion, that he should keep his own religion to himself and not to seek by himself and such as he entertaineth to pervert others'. In addition he specified a group of laity in the area whom he saw as patrons of Catholicism – Dr Berkely, a physician, 'an apostate from the true religion … having masses and meetings of priests in his house … [and] seeking to pervert whom he can, especially on their deathbeds'; James Farrell a merchant, 'the chief harbourer of priests and Jesuits, in whose house the masses are most usually said' and who had been excommunicated some eight or nine years before; Andrew Hadaway, an apostate, a malicious papist, who being driven out of Scotland for religion dwelleth at Strabane'; James Crawford, the Countess of Abercorn's agent, 'who having married a Protestant turned her to popery'; Robert Algeo, Sir George Hamilton's steward; and Claud Algeo 'a lewd pseudo-catholic'.

At a recent episcopal visitation, Downham said, presentments were made 'of many British recusants (people who refused to attend Church of Ireland services) and of the Master as the ringleader of them', and he expressed the opinion that 'if speedy course be not taken to suppress popish insolencies, it is much feared that the town of Strabane (the inhabitants whereof have their dependence upon him) will revolt, especially if the papists when they are driven out of Scotland may be received there as some have been'. The archbishop of Glasgow, he said, had protested to him for suffering 'them who are expelled out of Scotland for religion to be harboured within [his] diocese'. Bishop Downham also passed on the testimony of an informant that about May 1628 there had been a 'great meeting' of priests at Strabane, 'which priests were lodged at James Farrell's, so many as his house would hold, the rest dispersed here and there in the town'.

Despite the bishop's rhetoric, the numbers of Scots Catholics involved may not have been as great as might be expected. The only numerical data emerge from the statement of Downham's informant that 'Blackney useth to say mass twice every Sunday, the first at or near Strabane at James Farrell's or Robert Algeo's at which there use to be besides the Irish about forty Scottish, the second at Sir George Hamiltons'. These Scots Catholics were clearly from the Strabane area, and no doubt there were others elsewhere in the barony. If most of them lived in Strabane they have been no more than a substantial minority of its population, and clearly no 'mass house' had been set up. It seems certain, at any rate, that a number of those listed by name as Catholics lived in the town. James Farrell was of Strabane in 1626, and, as well as being a merchant, appears as a leaseholder on Sir George Hamilton of Greenlaw's estate in 1622. The doctor, Berkely, was more likely to live in town than countryside. Hadaway lived in the town; Crawford did not; members of the Algeo family lived there.

However that a Plantation town, designed to be a centre of strength and orthodoxy in the Plantation, should be developing in this way was clearly of concern to the bishop and clearly a concern he expected the Dublin

Algeo stone, Malison Bridge, Artigarvan

government to share. Hence he sent warrants to the provost of Strabane to arrest the clergy, MacSweeney, Blackney and O'Kelly, but was assured that 'he durst do nothing' for fear of antagonising the landlord. Downham's efforts, however, probably proved to be no more than a temporary, if severe, irritant. The bishop had complained bitterly in 1622 that the civil authorities were wanting in the prosecution of Catholic clergy throughout his diocese.

This now was indeed a time of intensified pressure on Catholicism – a proclamation against Roman jurisdiction was promulgated on 1 April 1629 – but the civil authorities, central and local, lacked the capacity and perhaps the resolution for a sustained onslaught. While at this time Downham considered the Dublin lords justices sympathetic to him, he was aware of his dependence on them, 'for the ecclesiastical authority in these parts without the assistance of the civil power is so weak that we seem to exercise a precary jurisdiction'. Around this period, 1628–30, there are numerous references to the presence of papists and Jesuits in the area. On one occasion Sir George Hamilton, Sir William Hamilton and Claud Hamilton are alleged to have attended a meeting in Strabane at which money was given to priests and Jesuits in order that agents might go to Rome. However it was thought that 'respectable' Catholics were hostile towards the Jesuits.

It is possible that many of the Protestants in the Strabane area, being a minority group, felt themselves endangered by the presence of so many Roman Catholics and this may have caused them to report on the activities of the Hamilton family and possibly have exaggerated them. Sir William Stewart certainly complained about the meeting which the Hamiltons attended at Strabane when priests and Jesuits were present. It is significant that the protests died down very quickly when peace was made with Spain in 1630.

With the preponderance of Catholics in the Strabane area it is highly unlikely that any of them left in 1639 when all Ulster Scots over 16 had to declare their disapproval of the 1638 Scottish National Covenant. This would also help account for the fact that none of the undertakers were murdered in Strabane during the native Irish rebellion of 1641, and that the same families, retained their land after the rebellion. James Hamilton, Lord Strabane, who was a minor at the time of the 1641 rebellion, later sided with the native Irish in 1650 against Oliver Cromwell's forces. The Civil Survey of the mid 1650s names all the Hamiltons as being papists and that the church in the parish of Camus-juxta-Mourne had been completed.

The fact that so many of the undertakers in Strabane barony were Roman Catholics does not seem to have hindered the progress of the Plantation, rather it seems to have aided it. Relations between the native Irish and the

Old Camus Church

undertakers would have been improved by the common bond of the Roman Catholic faith. It is tantalising that we can say little about Protestantism in Strabane in this period. In 1622 Bishop Downham in his visitation return (see next section for extracts covering all parishes in Strabane barony) indicated that he had united the two parishes of Leckpatrick and Camus-juxta-Mourne:

> This parish [Camus-juxta-Mourne] being small, and the town of Strabane built on the confines thereof, I united in the former incumbents' time these two parishes and think them fit to be united, the rather because there is a fair church begun by the late Earl of Abercorn intended to serve for these two contiguous parishes, howsoever that building of the church with the death of the earl hath ceased ...

It had been planned at the time of Plantation to create a new parochial organisation to coincide with the boundaries of the Plantation estates and although this had not been put into effect, Abercorn's church building and the bishop's uniting of the two parishes was a local move in this direction. However in 1622 the old church of Leckpatrick 'remained uncovered', and

Abercorn's building incomplete. At this time the incumbent of both parishes, Henry Noble, MA, 'a good preacher of competent learning and of good conversation', lived in the town of Strabane. Thereafter, however, difficulties arose, and the parishes appear to have been separate for ten years from 1626.

The building of the church in Strabane remained incomplete, no doubt through the disinterest of the Earl's Catholic successors, so that in 1634 John Browne, the provost, appealed to the bishop, John Bramhall, on behalf of 'the inhabitants of Strabane' for assistance concerning their church building. He stated that the larger parish of Leckpatrick 'upon which a great part of the town of Strabane standeth' opposed the building of one church for both parishes, and asked the bishop to have the uniting of the two parishes confirmed by parliament. Later Bishop Bramhall dismissed Noble from his cure of Camus-juxta-Mourne, according to a letter of the bishop's in 1641, for 'professed popery' – a commentary on the ambiguous position of Protestantism in Strabane at that time. The fact that there were three different clergy appointed to Camus-juxta-Mourne between 1636 and 1639 may indicate problems and tensions. Throughout the period the clergy of both parishes were predominantly English. As well as that we only get tiny glimpses of an apparently marginal Protestant dissent in the town at the end of our period.

RJH

1622 Visitation reports and list of incumbents

Ardstraw

Church is ruinous. Sir Robert Newcomen given a licence to build in another place (Newtownstewart) which yet has not begun (building commenced in 1623), the greatest part of the parish deeming the old church might be required. Meanwhile another place is provided for divine service. Valuation is £30 above one third of clear value, vicesima is 30 shillings. Three townlands of glebe belong to the parish, but one (called Fagernah) is detained by Sir Daniel Leigh (of Omagh). This was an example of church land obtained by a layman prior to the Plantation, which the parish still considered to belong to it. Incumbent discharges are by a sufficient preacher allowing him a stipend of £20.

Incumbents: 1617 11 March – John Richardson who was a Fellow of Trinity College, Dublin in 1593; in 1621 he became Dean of Derry and appointed a curate to Ardstraw.

1639 11 February – Richard Winter (died 1641).

Badoney

Church is ruinous. Incumbent is G. Walker who has dispensation to hold with Cappy. Value Kings Book £10 somewhat more than quarter clear value. Vicesima 10 shillings. Has one townland of Glebe set in wild mountainous country two miles from church. Incumbent has bound tenant to build house (in progress). Cure partly by himself and partly by Irish clerk, parish being wholly Irish recusants.

Badoney Graveyard, Glenelly Valley

Camus-juxta-Mourne

Church is ruinous. (It was never rebuilt. Today one sees one gable wall with the remaining walls standing at 3 feet. Internal measurements are approximately 66 ft x 18 ft. The entrance is by a gate at the original position of the door (about 200 people could have been seated in the church). Valuation is £3. 6s. 8d. which is one third of clear value, vicesima is 4d. This parish is small and the town of Strabane is built in the confines. United the two parishes (this one with Leckpatrick q.v.) because late Earl of Abercorn began to build a church to serve both parishes. However, building has stopped with death of the Earl.

Two townlands of glebe, nothing built on them.

Incumbent lives in Strabane where he discharges the cures.

Incumbents: 1620 Alexander Spicer

                 1622 Henry Noble MA (also Leckpatrick)

                 1636 24 April – William Kingsmill

                 1638 30 July – Leonard Kempe (to Ballinascreen)

                 1639 9 November – Robert Semple

Former parish church of Cappagh, Dunmullan

Cappagh

Church is ruinous. Incumbent a grave man and an ancient preacher. Valuation in Kings Book is £13. 6s. 8d., third part above value. Vicesima is 13s. 4d. It has three townlands of glebe. On one called Rehan incumbent has built one mansion after the English fashion. Incumbent is resident and serveth the cure himself in a house given by Sir J. Drummond for that purpose.

Incumbent: G. Walker (BA Dublin 1621; MA 1624; 1633, DD). Also confirmed in position on 26 September, 1636; held Badoney parish in addition.

Donagheady

Church walls built but no roof. Valuation is £20 which one third of the clear value. Three townlands of glebe. Upon one there is a stone house or castle formerly.

Incumbents: 1622 Robert Semple MA – an honest man and preacher is resident and discharges the cure in his own person.

1635 1 September – Edward Stanhope, who died in 1642 of fever during rebellion.

Leckpatrick

Remaineth uncovered. Valuation is £16 which is about one third of clear value. Vicesima is 16 shillings.

Incumbents: 1622 Henry Noble MA – good preacher and competent of learning and of a good conversation.

1625 5th December – Alexander Spicer.

1636 22nd April – William Kingsmill (plus Urney).

1638 6th March – Richard Wakefield.

Urney

Church remaynth ruinous although the Lord Primate has granted necessary fund for its repair. Valuation £8. 6s. 8d. which is one third clear value. Vicesima 13s. 3d. Glebe is townland plus half besides a fort detained by Richard Babington from him. There are some buildings on the glebe but the incumbent being a single man lyveth in a gentleman's house near the church and performeth the cure in his own person.

Incumbents: 1617 12 November – Isaac Wood M.A.

                1637 31 January – William Kingsmill (also held Leckpatrick).

Mrs M Mrs McG
JMC IW

Hamilton monument in Old Leckpatrick Graveyard

5

Military Matters in Troubled Times

The period under review began and ended with a guerrilla war. In the 1590s the Ulster chiefs met with various misfortunes at the hands of the English throughout Ireland, with a few successes such as the victory at the Yellow Ford in 1598. Reverses in 1600 saw the fighting confined to the North. In May of that year Sir Henry Docwra occupied Derry with orders to attack the chiefs from the North and to separate O'Neill from O'Donnell by establishing forts along the Foyle. Local chiefs such as Sir Arthur O'Neill (son of Turlough Luineach), Niall Garbh O'Donnell (of Castlefinn) and Donnell O'Cahan (lord of north County Coleraine) were successively bought over.

During this early part of our survey what was happening in the Strabane barony? The building of forts along the Foyle was noteworthy. Greencastle (an old Norman Castle), Culmore and Derry in the lower reaches of Lough Foyle followed by Dunalong (opposite a small O'Donnell fort at Carrigans) and Lifford (the Liffer) in the upper reaches. The maps on the following pages of the forts established by English troops at Lifford and Dunalong *c.* 1601 give some idea of the building operations that took place. In 1601 Lifford had some 80 houses – Strabane still lay in ruins after the fighting that had taken place earlier. This fighting was basically of a guerrilla type. In November 1600 Niall Garbh's brother had attacked Harry Ovingdon (O'Neill's foster brother) at Island McHugh, taking away 500 cows and some horses. In the following March the garrison at Lifford burnt Newtown, captured 200

Omagh fort, early 1600s

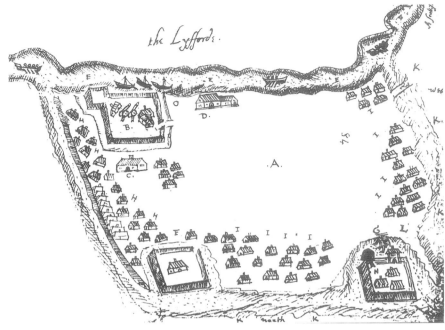

Lifford fort *c*. 1601

cows with 100 persons 'put to the sword'. Later the same month Docwra sent soldiers 'to side', captured 300 cows, but lost all but 40 due to bad weather and unfordable rivers.

Early in 1601 Cormac O'Neill (Sir Arthur O'Neill's brother) had fortified Strabane after being given tools to rebuild the settlement by Docwra. Local people brought 5,000 cows to Strabane (as a form of tribute) which were transferred by Docwra to Inishowen. However, Docwra suspected Cormac O'Neill of double dealing. He ordered O'Cahan to attack Strabane. This took place on 27 May 1601. However, O'Cahan lost four men to O'Neill's one. On the same day Niall Garbh repelled an attack on Lifford launched by O'Donnell who had been observed a week previously to have had 800 men 12 miles above Lifford.

The number of men available at the forts varied. Returns given showed that in December 1600 there were 1,300 foot and 50 horse at Derry; 1,050 foot at Dunalong; and 950 foot and 50 horse at Lifford. In April 1601 Dunalong and Lifford numbers had been reduced by half, but, offset by Niall Garbh having available 500 foot and 100 horse. However, Docwra was still unsure of both Niall Garbh's and Cormac O'Neill's allegiance to the crown. He obtained pledges of support in June. In August he spread his Irish supporters around his area after having made a show of strength at Strabane.

Dunalong fort *c.* 1601

Niall Garbh sent to Donegal half of Cormac O'Neill's men (100) with Cormac himself to the heart of the O'Donnell country; 50 men to Turlough Maguylson at Newtown and 50 men to Art McHugh Mergoh at Omagh. Docwra was complaining of the shortage of men. He had sent 650 to Donegal, had 507 sick, and needed over 700 to bring the garrison up to full strength. By this time the Spanish invasion scares had become more of a reality, for during August a Spanish ship was chased from Lough Foyle to Sligo. Late September saw Spanish ships off Kinsale and two months later O'Neill and O'Donnell arrived with an army of 6,000 men and 500 horse and, as a result of mismanagement, were defeated on Christmas Eve, 1601. During this period Docwra was still keeping an eye on the local chiefs who had not joined O'Neill and O'Donnell on their southward march. At the end of November he had made a sortie into O'Cahan country burning houses and corn, capturing sheep and garrons, killing many, including O'Cahan's brother Rory.

There was one further episode in the struggle between the Irish chiefs and the English, after the Flight of the Earls, which affected the Strabane area. This was the rebellion in April 1608 of Sir Cahir O'Dogherty, the Lord of Inishowen. He had become exasperated with the behaviour of the governor of Derry, Sir George Paulet. He attacked the fort at Culmore on the 18th and sacked Derry the next day, and went on to burn Strabane. He continued to harass the various garrisons but these had been able to subdue him by June, just before some 200 Scots recruits who had been sent by the government arrived at Carrickfergus. Niall Garbh was reputedly the real instigator of the revolt and for this he ended his days in the Tower of London.

These events saw the end of a period of spasmodic guerrilla warfare which had continued with varying degrees of intensity for almost 20 years. Over 30 years were to elapse before the next rising of the Gael in 1641. However, during this period all undertakers had to provide their own force of men for protection. Muster rolls were maintained with periodic listings being made. Newtownstewart was the muster centre for the area. The only record found for Strabane barony was that for 1630. A summary is given in the table below. For a full list of names refer to *Ardstraw – Historical Survey of a Parish 1600–1900* by John H. Gebbie (1968). It will be seen that nearly half the men listed lived in Strabane and that over a fifth had no arms.

MUSTER ROLL FOR 1630

	Men	Muskets	Swords	Snaphances	Pikes	Calivers	Halberts	No arms
Town of Strabane	208	4	139	51	44	11	2	63
Sir Wm Hamilton	43	–	42	18	22	1	–	1
Countess of Abercorn	40	–	36	12	7	1	–	4
Master of Abercorn	51	1	39	16	10	1	–	10
Sir George Hamilton	54	–	47	16	12	2	1	3
Sir William Stewart	54	8	32	5	10	9	1	16
Malcolm Drummond	15	–	15	2	11	1	–	–
	465	13	350	120	116	26	4	97

Summary table covering the 'Town of Strabane' and the areas of each landlord

The 1641 rising was planned by the native Irish chiefs who had been allocated land in south Tyrone. They no doubt still had many sympathisers in Strabane barony from which many of them had been ejected. One of the Irish protagonists was Sir Phelim O'Neill who would, in 1649, marry Lord Strabane's widow.

On 23 October 1641 (the first full day of the uprising) Newtownstewart was attacked and burnt by the rebels with Strabane suffering a similar fate shortly afterwards. Although guerrilla type activities developed – in fact they continued throughout the 1640s – the Strabane area seems to have missed most of the fighting.

The forts of Derry and Enniskillen were the main defence bases, and there was some communication between them. In addition, Sir William Stewart of Newtownstewart played a leading role, his castle being a refuge for local settlers.

After 1642 Ireland's war became part of the British Royalist versus Parliament struggle. In the northwest, the Stewarts, Sir William of Newtownstewart and Sir Robert, organised what was known as the Laggan Army.

In the late spring of 1646, the Stewarts marched towards south Tyrone to join up with General Monro, who had been in northeast Ulster since April 1642. The intention was to encircle the rebels, but Owen Roe O'Neill defeated them at Benburb on 5 June. Again, for various reasons, the opportunity to press home their advantage was lost. A year later the Parliamentarians gained a base at Dublin where Cromwell arrived with an army in August 1649. Irish resistance did not end until 1652, but before that we note that in July 1650 James Hamilton, Lord Strabane, had fought with Sir Phelim O'Neill at Charlemont and had fled to the woodlands of central Tyrone after the fort had fallen.

Small armies of rebels still roamed Ulster and they were finally subdued at Scarrifhollis near Letterkenny in June 1651. Thus, we see that the period of our survey started and ended with a guerrilla war situation.

JMC

6

Economic Aspects

General background to 1610

The native Irish economy in Ulster in 1600 was basically self sufficient. A surplus of cattle and some crops led to a limited amount of trading with Scotland. However, the garrisons along the Foyle were mostly provisioned by sea by the merchants of Chester. Reports of the raids launched by Docwra against the local chiefs often noted that some hundreds of cows had been captured. At one time 16,000 were impounded in Inishowen. Beer was produced at Dunalong for the forts on the Foyle, being transported to them by boats.

The provisions brought into Derry included oatmeal, rice, butter, cheese, bacon and pork. Noteworthy was reference to Newland (Newfoundland) fish and Holland ling (Dutch fishing boats fished off Western Scotland). However, the difficulties of shipping supplies so far must have contributed to the problems encountered in maintaining the health of the soldiers. At one time a fifth were sick. In 1601 Queen Elizabeth issued a proclamation making 3d. pass for 1/–, hence the difficulty in buying anything from merchants in Ulster, which no doubt added to the problems. The chicanery of merchants and the muster masters (the men who in effect looked after the administration of the garrisons) also added to the difficulties of obtaining food and materials for building forts, houses and wharves. An example was the increase in the price of beer from £6 per ton at Chester to £16, the price paid by men at Derry (2d. per quart).

Lough Foyle was the main trade route of the area. Boats of 200 tons could navigate as far as Dunalong. Three miles further the channel becomes narrow with islands and then fordable in many places, and navigable at high tide for 'barks' of 20 tons as far as Lifford.

The fishing on Lough Foyle was extremely important. There were a number of well known pools which became subject to disputes between the bishops of Derry and the Irish Society after the Plantation, although until the Plantation the King had granted the fishery (plus those of the River Bann and Lough Neagh) to James Hamilton of Bangor (and seven others). The amount of 3 ½ tons of salmon was said to be caught on behalf of this group on Lough Foyle by net between June and the end of August. Local people also fished for trout and flounders. In winter the river provided meat in the form of wild swans, geese, ducks, teal, herons, cranes, plovers and seagulls.

In the first decade of the 17th century travellers along the river would have seen birch woods, with coppice wood on the islands. Around Lifford and Strabane there was open country with some woodland and cultivation. If the pattern of Inishowen was repeated here they would have seen flax, oats and barley in open fields with no enclosures, together with cows, horses, sheep and swine.

JMC

Income and expenditure

An undertaker had to pay the King an annual rent of £5 6s. 8d. per 1,000 acres (a small proportion). What rent was paid to the undertaker by his tenants? Only one small record has survived for Strabane barony. This is a rental for the proportions of Eden and Killeny for the years 1613–15. Also included are items of expenditure for the same period, the whole forming part of the financial accounts prepared following the death of Sir Claud Hamilton in October 1614.

The table on the following page covers the rental returns for the Killeny proportion. It has been possible to relate the areas given in the original document to present day townlands – in fact most townland names in that district have not altered since the Plantation. The rent comprised three parts: money; service by the tenant on behalf of the undertaker, and the provision of agricultural goods. Taken together some idea of the productivity of particular townlands can be gauged. How did the undertaker (or his agent) dispose of the agricultural items? If the Eden and Killeny produce was sold the money raised does not appear in the accounts. Did barter take place between landlords, or did an undertaker or his agent only expect to receive goods and service when resident? A monetary value for goods and service was

Townlands (modern names)	Modern-size Townlands in acres	Tenants
Moneycannon (would include Ballyneaner, Liscloon and Ballynacross)	1,827	Hew Don O'Duffom[b]
Killyclooney, Glencosh, Killycurry[c] (would include Windy Hill)	1,427	Oone O'Mory – 1613[d] Kilglafid(?) O'Duffeme and Oone O'Mory – 1614
Stoneyfalls and Donemana (originally 2/3 Binelly)	254	
Leat, Ballaghalare (would include Gobnascale)	504	Claud Hamilton
Drumman, Tirkernaghan (would include Barran)	1,543	Patrick Groome O'Duffeme
Tirconnolly (would include Carnagribben, Claggan and Gortaclare)	1,385	Patrick Groome O'Duffeme
Aughtermoy, Killenny	459	Patrick Groome O'Duffeme and Philomye O'Duffemi
Rousky, Drain (would include Lisnaragh)	951	Brian Crou O'Duffeme[g]
	8,350	

FOOTNOTES
a   Rental period was 'from Alhallowtyde till Alhallowtyde'.
b   In the two years was unable to pay £6. 6. 0.
c   In 1613/14 Killycurry was given by Sir Claud to Dr Robert Hamilton – no rent charged.

RENTAL 1612/13[a]

£ Money	Service – days	Beere [barley] – barrels	Sheep	Pigs	Hens and capons	Butter – barrels
10	16	–	–	–	–	–
10	24	4	3	3	18	–
W A S T E						
10	24	4	4	2	24	–
20	18[e]	8	8	8	36	1[f]

Waste to May 1613 then set to May 1614

£ Money	Service – days	Beere [barley] – barrels	Sheep	Pigs	Hens and capons	Butter – barrels
9	16	4	4	4	16	–[f]
6	16	4	4	–	16	–
9	32	6	10	10	24	–
74	146	30	33	27	134	1

RENTAL 1613/14[a]

£ Money	Service – days	Beere [barley] – barrels	Sheep	Pigs	Hens and capons	Butter – barrels
W A S T E						
12	24	4	4	4	18	–
W A S T E						
'Plenishit with Sir Claud's own goods' (cattle)						
20	18[e]	8	8	8	36	1[f]
May to Nov. 1614 – Waste						
6	16	4	4	4	16	–
12	24	6	10	10	24	–
50	82	22	26	26	94	1

FOOTNOTES
d   In the two years was unable to pay £4.
e   Provided a horse as well as a man.
f   Rent included a 4 year old cow and calf.
g   In the two years was unable to pay £6. 10. 0.

not taken into account by the agent in 1615 when both proportions were let to Patrick Groome O'Duffeme (later O'Devin) for £220. This compares with the money rent of £257 10s. 0d. for 1613 and £162 2s. 6d. for 1614.

Sir Claud farmed Leat and Ballaghalare himself in 1613 and 1614 so the entry for 1613 is academic. The comptar (accountant) deducted the £10 rent in the accounts, and paid the 'heard' (cattleman) £3 for looking after the cattle for the year. At the end of April 1614 the cattle were sold. (For details see page 65.) The stock comprised one bull, 37 cows, 5 calves, 17 stirks and 9 oxen, and was sold for £58 17s. 8d.

In the accounts one finds that a number of tenants were excused payment of money due to Sir Claud. Ten men were excused payment of £70 16s. 0d. Seven of these were tenants in Eden owing £52 10s, with three in Killeny owing £18 6s. 0d.

There is no doubt that Patrick Groome O'Duffeme was a useful man where Sir Claud and his successors were concerned. Not only was he able to take on the collection of rents for the two proportions in 1615, but he also took £23 10s. to Sir Claud (presumably living in Scotland) in November 1613, he was also paid 23/– 'for fetching a horse from Eden left there by Art Stewart'.

The total income for the three years was £708 10s. 2d. (this included the sale of the cattle referred to above), whilst the expenditure (discharges) set against this is £662 3s. 8d. There is little information on what happened to the money once it had reached Sir Claud, his agents or successor. Some examples of payments:

May 1613	Sent with James Elphinstonn to Scotland to be given be him to Sir Claud – £56.
August 1613	To James Hamilton for services to umquill (the late) Sir Claud – £15.
November 1613	Delivered by David Stewart to Sir Claud. – £26 2s 5d.
December 1613	And sent with Michaell Kar to Sir Claud – £20.
May 1614	And sent with Johne Nasmythe to Sir Claud. – £40.
23 May 1614	And to the collections of the King's rent for the payment at Michalmes 1614 – £5 6s 8d.
	To Gilbert McCraken, millar for meill (meal) furnishit be him to heard (cattleman) in Lait – 22/–

Payed to Mr Borrisford in Colrane for the repayment of money borrowit fur Sir Claud from the Lonndanary at Londonn – £50.

Sent with Robert Algeo to Scotland which was to delivrit to Algeo and Inglis – £50.

To the comptar (accountant) restis for complating of his charge ye sowme off £46 10s. (the accountant's fee).

The only items of expenditure within the Strabane barony noted was the purchase of the meal for the cattle, a wage to the cattleman and the cost of building the castle, bawn and gate house, a total of £148 5s. (See page 75.)

JMC

Development of the land

From the rental table for 1613 and 1614 it can be seen that the Moneycannon–Tirconnolly area was almost a write off. This might well explain why Hew Don O'Duffom was unable to pay most of the rent in 1613 for Moneycannon. Perhaps Patrick Groome O'Duffeme was able to demonstrate to Hamilton's agent that Tirconnolly was incapable of producing any rent in 1614. Land in the lower part of the Burndennet valley (Killyclooney–Killycurry district), and even higher up (Rousky–Drumman) produced good rents with Patrick Groome O'Duffeme leasing the most land – over a third of the total acreage. In 1614 Oone O'Mory had to pay a little more in cash and provide another sheep and pig from the Killyclooney–Killycurry lands.

The table on the next page lists the same townlands in the Killeny proportion and shows their value and land use as noted in the 1654–6 Civil Survey which endeavoured to recall the situation in 1641 at the time of the armed uprising. From this table some idea can be obtained of the extent of land capable of producing an income. It is assumed that 'shrubby and mountain' land was used for rough grazing and hence considered to be income producing. From the areas given it would seem that land above 400 feet was still in a natural wild state and no attempt had been made to make it productive.

Townlands (in the same order as the 1612–1614 rental list)	£ Value	Survey land use in Irish acres					Size of townlands		Actual
							Survey		
		Arable	Pasture	Meadow	Shrubby	Mountain	Irish Acres	Statute Acres	Statute Acres
Moneycannon (with Ballyneaner, Liscloon and Ballynacross)	241	70	100	–	–	100	370	600	3,212 (A)
Killyclooney (with Windy Hill)	22	70	20	2	25	88	205	332	919
Glencosh	5	30	–	–	10	50	90	146	356
Killycurry	5	30	4	–	8	38	80	130	152
Stoneyfalls and Donemana	7	25	–	–	–	32	57	92	254
Leat (with Ballaghalare and Gobnascale)	6	40	–	–	6	34	90	146	604
Drumman	10	40	–	–	6	54	100	162	337
Tirkernaghan	7	50	30	–	5	75	160	259	910
Barran	5	20	–	–	4	46	70	113	296
Tirconnolly (with Carnagribben, Gortaclare and Claggan)	(A)	Included in Moneycannon above							
Aughtermoy	6	40	–	–	4	36	80	130	235
Killenny	6	30	8	–	–	42	80	130	224
Rousky	8	50	10	–	20	20	100	162	325
Drain	4	15	5	–	–	27	47	76	455
Lisnaragh	3	12	2	–	4	8	26	42	171

By 1641 it will be seen that a fifth of the Moneycannon–Tirconnolly area, the highest area of Killeny, was being 'farmed' whereas most of Killycurry in the lowest part of the Burndennet valley was capable of producing an income. Townlands on which about half the area was profitable included Rousky, Killeny, Aughtermoy and Drumman. The monetary value of the whole proportion in 1641 was £118 compared with the 'cash' proportion of the rent in 1613 of £74 and £50 a year later.

The names of only two tenants in 1631 were found. Shane Roe O'Devin had a sub lease of Moneycannon from James Hamilton and Patrick Groome O'Devin a sub lease from Thomas Pettegrew in Leat. Is the latter the same man who was the leading tenant in the 1613/5 period? He also rented Lough Ash nearby in the Eden proportion. Earlier Pynnar had noted that in the combined proportions there were six freeholders and fourteen leaseholders of British extraction. Three years later, it was reported that there were no British, but only 120 Irish families. Although 43 men are noted in the 1630 muster roll on Sir William Hamilton's land, which included Eden and Killeny, no clue as to where these men lived or what role they played in the settlements or countryside can be found.

SALE OF COWS FROM THE LANDS OF LEAT AT THE END OF APRIL 1614

		£	s	d
Sold to:	George Hamilton one cow and stirk	1	5	0
	John Stodart 10 cows @ 26/8	13	6	8
	Robert Hamilton one cow and calf	1	4	0
	William Midcalff six cows	7	19	0
	John Richie four cows with oalfs and stirk	5	6	8
	A cow to John Richie	1	4	0
	Ane Inglis four cows	4	12	0
	John Dunning two cows	2	6	0
	Another cow to him	1	3	0
	For nine oxen	9	0	0
	For seven cows @ 23/4	8	3	4
	For a bull	8	0	0
	For year old unlibbet (ungelded) stirks – 15 @ 4/–	3	0	0
		58	17	8

JMC

Trade at the beginning of the Plantation

When the Plantation started undertakers were permitted to import livestock. For a large proportion (2,000 acres) the limits were 120 cows, 2 bulls, 20 young stores, 100 ewes, 6 rams, 20 mares, horses or colts and not more than 10 swine. There is no evidence that any of the undertakers in Strabane barony brought livestock with them or imported them later. However, Pynnar's survey of 1618/9 reported 'that the Earl of Abercorn had 120 cows whilst his tenants had 80 cows and 16 garrons between them.

A small amount of trade existed between Scotland and Ulster before the Plantation. Exports consisted of yarn, cow hides, with some oats, barley, timber and fish. Imports included fish, coal and whisky. No records have survived to enable this to be quantified. After 1611 information can be obtained for Derry (and Strabane) from the Derry port book 1612–15, and is discussed in chapter 12 of Michael Perceval-Maxwell's *The Scottish Migration to Ulster in the Reign of James I* (1973).

The few individual references in the Derry port book to the Strabane barony undertakers are given below. It seems likely that small boats such as the *Gift of God* of Strabane operated from Strabane directly.

25 March 1614	Exports to Glasgow in the *Jennet* by William Hamilton value £71 18s. and by Sir George Hamilton value £9 2s. 6d.
8 April 1614	Imports from Renfrew in the *Katherine* of Renfrew by the Earl of Abercorn value £9 4s. 8d.
14 June 1614	Exports to Renfrew in the *George* of Renfrew by the Earl of Abercorn value £17 13s. 4d.
15 July 1614	Imports in the *Gift of God* of Strabane (xx ton burthen) by Robert Lindsiee (Master) value £4.18s.
25 July 1614	Imports in the *William* of Renfrew by the Earl of Abercorn value £2 14s.
23 August 1614	Exports to the Clyde on the *Gift of God* of Strabane by Earl of Abercorn value £186 13s. 4d. and by Matthew Lindsiee value £10 7s. 6d.
?	Imports in 'a small boat from Scotland' by Hugh Hamilton value £34
21 September 1614	Imports in the *Gift of God* of Strabane by Matthew Lindsiee value £2 5s.

25 September 1614	Exports in 'a small boat from Scotland' to Scotland by the Earl of Abercorn value £12 11s. 8d. and by John Hamilton value £7 2s. 6d.
9 November 1614	Exports to Renfrew by John Bersban 5 cwt cheese value £1 13s. 4d. and 3 vessels of butter, 3 cwt value £2
27 January 1615	Imports in the *Gift of God* of Strabane by Matthew Lindsiee 12 tons of coal value £3 and 1 ton of salt value 16s. 0d.
27 February 1615	Exports to Renfrew included some sent by William Hamilton (Strabane?).
?	Imports from Renfrew included some for John Browne (Strabane?).
?	Imports from Glasgow included coal for Sir William Stewart.
8 April 1615	Exports in the *Gift of God* of Strabane included goods sent by the Earl of Abercorn.
9 May 1615	Imports in the *Gift of God* of Strabane by Robert Lindsiee 20 tons of coal value £5
12 May 1615	Imports included goods for John Kennedie (Strabane?).

Other exports in 1615 not quantified included oats, oatmeal, barley and hides.

JMC, RJH

7
Buildings

Buildings before the Plantation

At the time of the Plantation the normal type of house was the single storey thatched cottage. Throughout Ireland there was a variety of design not only in the layout of the house but also in the roofing materials. The type of building in the northwest of Ireland was quite distinctive. From the sketches of buildings seen on contemporary maps of the area it can be seen that houses were of a long rectangular shape, sometimes with an outshot on one side. The fire was in one gable wall with a partition screening off a section to form a separate bedroom. The outshot would have contained a dresser bed. Frequently the house would have had two doors opposite each other.

The roof was normally carried on purlins resting on coupled rafters, traditionally of oak (bog oak if available in areas where oak trees

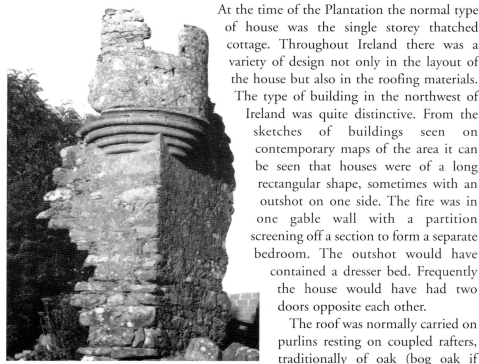

Ruin of Mountcastle, near Dunnamanagh

were scarce). The roof was rounded, with the thatch retained by horizontal and vertical ropes of twisted straw or bog fir secured to the walls by stone pegs.

None of these have survived in the Strabane area although some outhouses on farms in the more remote areas may show some of the features described. Similarly no complete non domestic buildings have survived. The two main groups here are churches and castles. Of the churches, only the remains of walls are to be seen at Camus, with even less at other sites. Similarly for the castles and forts. Although the fort at Dunalong had a short life its outline can be seen on the 1834 6-inch Ordnance Survey map. Today the site is covered by a farm.

Castles suffered a similar fate with over building taking place at Strabane and Newtownstewart. Traces can be seen at Mountcastle, Island McHugh and the nearby loughside. The only substantial remnant is 'Harry Avery's Castle' traditionally associated with Henry Aimhreidh O'Neill who died in 1391. It is built on a prominence about one mile southwest of Newtownstewart, where it commands a wide view of the valley of the River Mourne. It was designed after the fashion of the 'double D' towered gatehouse originating in the 13th century which can also be seen at Carrickfergus and Castleroche, near Dundalk. It is probably a 14th–century structure.

IW

Building progress during the Plantation – the surveys

Every undertaker who had a proportion of 2,000 acres was to build 'a stone house with a strong court or bawn about it. Every undertaker with a proportion of 1,500 acres had to fulfil the same conditions, but the house might be of brick instead of stone. Those with 1,000 acres did not have to build a house, but they did have to build a court or bawn. They were to have the building work carried out within three years of Easter 1611. The undertakers were also responsible for ensuring that their tenants erected family dwellings close by their own house and bawn as an aid to mutual defence and in an attempt to establish towns and villages.

A check on the progress of the undertakers in fulfilling these building conditions was a principal aim of each of the government surveys carried out during the early years of the plantation. These were undertaken by Sir George Carew, 1611; Sir Josias Bodley, 1613; Captain Nicholas Pynnar, 1618/9; and by commissioners, including Sir Nathaniel Rich, 1622.

When Carew made his survey in 1611, James Haig and Sir Claud Hamilton had not yet appeared in Ulster, so there had been nothing done on their proportions at Tirenemuriertagh and at Killeny and Eden. Sir Thomas Boyd had done nothing on his proportion, but he was reported to be preparing the materials for building. Sir John Drummond, James Clapham and George Hamilton were all in Strabane on their proportions, but they were in a similar position to Sir Thomas Boyd. These men had all been in Ulster for a few months at the most, and it is not surprising that they had little built for it must have taken time to provide building materials and recruit men to carry out the construction work. Carew noted that Sir George Hamilton had built a strong timber house. However, it was the Earl of Abercorn who had made most progress, no doubt made possible by having been sent 25 men at the behest of the King in May 1611. No other undertaker received such assistance. Abercorn's achievements at this early stage are quite impressive and presumably was cited as an example of meeting the Plantation conditions.

Carew noted that Abercorn 'has built for the present near the town of Strabane some large timber houses and a court 116 foot in length and 87 foot in breadth, the grounsells of oak and timber and the rest of alder and birch, which is well thatched with heath and finished. Has built a great brew house without his court 46 foot long and 25 foot wide'. He was also preparing to build a castle and a bawn in the following year, and had encouraged his tenants to build for themselves. Before May 1611 they had built 32 houses of 'fayre coples' (inclined rafters) and by the autumn another 28 had been constructed.

The survey carried out by Sir Josias Bodley in 1613 adds little to the information on the development of Strabane. It seems likely that after the initial efforts of building both Abercorn and his tenants needed a year or two to consolidate what had been achieved. Pynnar's survey (1618/9) however shows that more building work had been undertaken, though it is not possible to say exactly when it was carried out.

Abercorn, at Strabane, had built a 'strong castle', but not a bawn. This broke one of the conditions of the Plantation but it was probably not required in this embryo town. A school house of lime and stone had been built and a church had been started. However, its building was stopped in March 1618 when Abercorn died, with the walls standing 5 feet high. The town now consisted of 80 houses, many of lime and stone, plus other timber houses. Three water mills had also been built.

Later in the 1622 survey we see that 'there are above 100 dwelling houses diverse of them of stone and lyme'. It is implied that the church was completed, but this was not the case (see 1622 church visitation reports above). There was a 'sessionhouse and a market cross of stone and lime with a strong room under it to keep prisoners in (until they can be conveniently conducted to his majesty's gaol at Dungannon) and a platform on top which is a place of good defence'. Only one mill is noted, but it had a bridge over the waters alongside.

Between 1613 and 1618 Abercorn acquired Sir Thomas Boyd's proportion of Shean. Since Boyd had displayed little interest in his land it is unlikely that he had done any building work before he disposed of his proportion. Abercorn soon commenced building work and Pynnar reported that the castle had been started and was due to be completed by the following summer (1619). However, in the 1622 survey we find that the construction of the castle had only reached the second storey. The size of bawn reported to Pynnar was to be 80 feet square with four flankers, Rich noted that work had begun (on) a bawn of lime and stone, 48 foot long, 42 foot broad and 4 foot high with one small flanker covered with thatch in which Mr Robert Hamilton and his wife do dwell'. It was reported that there were 7 or 8 creats (basic native cabins) adjoining the site of the castle.

Abercorn had obviously concentrated most of his efforts at Strabane, for Pynnar reported that on the Dunalong proportion there was 'neither castle nor bawn, but, upon some places of the land there are three or four good houses built of lime and stone (built) by the tenants'. These were no doubt the three good stone houses built by Hugh Hamilton, James Hamilton and William Lynn noted three years later. By 1622 there was 'a good castle of stone and lime, 3 stories high, but no body at this time dwelling in it; and about it a bawn 54 foot long, 42 foot broad and 6 foot high with two open flankers, but there is no gate to the bawn'.

Such differences when comparing the reports of the surveyors are found on other proportions. The development of building work on these is given below:

Largie

1611	Sir George Hamilton and family resident in a timber house 62 foot long and 30 foot wide. Has built a bawn and good timber houses for some families of Scots who came over with him.
1613	His house was near 60 Irish houses or cabins (could this have been Ballymagorry?). He was gathering materials, including lime, for further building work.
1618/9	No more building work on the house or bawn carried out, but he has built a village of 30 Irish coupled houses (could this have been Artigarvan?).

Derrywoon Castle, Barons Court

1622   Sir George had now 'built a good bawn of lime and stone, 99 foot
            long, 57 foot broad and (about) 8 foot high, with 4 flankers,
            upon two whereof are built two little store houses of stone and
            lime, covered with slate wherein Sir George and his lady with
            their family do usually inhabit. But they being in Scotland it is
            kept by their servants. Near adjoining to this is a town of 20
            houses inhabited by Scots'.

Eden and Killeny

1611   Sir Claud Hamilton had not appeared – nothing done.
1613   Sir Claud had still not appeared or made arrangements
            for building.
1618/9   Following the death of Sir Claud in October 1614 (he had only
            just arrived in Ulster), Sir George Hamilton administered the pro-
            portion. Pynnar found a bawn of lime and stone 70 foot square,
            14 foot high and a good castle in it. 6 small houses had been built
            near the bawn and divers other on the land.

Newtownstewart Castle

| 1622 | The castle was 4 storeys high covered with slate, with no windows or doors. Only a piece of a bawn which is not finished. (See next section.) |

Dirrywoon

1611	George Hamilton was resident and making provision for building.
1613	Taken over by Sir George Hamilton (owner of Largie).
1618/9	By then there was a bawn of lime and stone 60 feet square, 14 feet high with four flankers, two having 'very good lodgings in them'. Nearby was a village with 10 houses.
1622	Again the size given for the bawn is different – 90 foot long, 70 foot broad and 14 foot high. Within the bawn and taking up most of the space was an almost complete four storey stone house. Sir George intended to live in it when finished.

Newton and Lislap

| 1611 & 1613 | James Clapham resident in a sufficient house and bawn which he found ready built at Newton. Sold to Sir Robert Newcomen in 1614 or 1615. |
| 1618/9 | Sir Robert rebuilt the castle which is now four stories high and |

ready for the roof. Two sides of the 16 foot high bawn completed and the other two sides going up apace. A town was being
built by the castle – 14 houses already built.

1622   The castle now complete. The bawn measured 81 foot long, 66
foot broad, 9 foot high with two flankers, one not yet finished.
(See next section).

Ballymagoieth

1611   Sir John Drummond had taken possession in person. 9 or 10
& 1613   households settled on his land.

1618/9   'Upon this there is a bawn of lime and stone, 100 feet square with
four flankers; and in it a timber house of cage work, himself and
family dwelling therein'. A quarter of a mile away was a village of
10 houses and a water mill for corn.

1622   Again differences in measurement: the bawn measures '84 foot
long, 75 foot broad, in some place 6, in some place 10 foot high,
with 3 flankers; on 2 whereof are built two small stone houses,
slated. Within the bawn there is a house being of clay and stone
and thatched'.

Tirenemuriertagh

1611   James Haig did not appear – passed to Sir William Stewart and
Sir Claud Hamilton in 1612.

1618/9   Nothing built but expected to start in 1619.

1622   Sir George Hamilton (successor to Sir Claud Hamilton) had
built a bawn of lime and stone. 42 foot square, 7 foot high with
no flankers. The building of a castle within the bawn had reached
a height of 5 foot – no gates to the bawn. Sir Robert Newcomen,
who by then had the other half, had carried out no building
work.

There is virtually no information on the progress of building after 1622.
Later reports, such as the inquisitions and Civil Survey, describe only the
chief buildings on the estates, which match those discussed above.

IW JMC
Mrs M Mrs McG

Costs of building

Only one set of accounts giving details of building costs in Strabane barony have been found. Included in the Eden and Killeny rental accounts is basic information on the building of 'ane houis and barnis and get houis for performanis of the plantacionne'. Here is the first query – has the comptar (accountant) confused the word 'bawn' with barn. It must surely be the case. The account is dated 12 January 1618, so it can be concluded that the work had been completed in the previous year. Unfortunately, no clue is given regarding the date when building commenced.

The 1622 survey refers to a castle of lime and stone, 4 storeys high covered with slate wherein no body now dwells. There are no windows or doors. Only a piece of a bawn about it which is not finished. Had it been finished? When the castle became unoccupied did 17th century vandals move in and take away the stones to build houses or other buildings for themselves?

James Miller, mason, was paid £50 for building the house, barn (bawn) and gatehouse. The cost of quarrying the stones, burning the lime and cutting the timber (in the woods) – £23. 'For building of ane lyme kill which in all the lyme was burnt – 30/–'. For transporting all the stones, timber, sand and lime – £21. For preparing all the timber for joists, spans, doors, windows, staircases – £38. For all the hardware of the house; tools; planks and barrels (hoggats) for the scaffold etc – £10 13s. 0d. This gives a total coat of £144 3s.

The only other building cost known for Strabane barony is that reported by Sir Robert Newcomen, The rebuilding of the 4-storey castle at Newton, the construction of the bawn and (14 or 20?) houses cost £400. The two castles and bawn were similar in size but we do not have any details on the amount and type of accommodation within either building. (Would archaeological research provide the answers?). If building costs were similar at both locations then the cost of the houses would be of the order of £12 to £18.

JMC

Bibliography

This short bibliography lists those publications and documents consulted by members of the extra-mural class. For an extensive coverage readers should consult the book *The Scottish Migration to Ulster in the Reign of James I* by Michael Perceval-Maxwell (1973).

Manuscript sources

Bodleian Library – Carte MSS
British Library – MSS 4756, 4770
Huntingdon & Peterborough Record Office – Kimbolton MSS
Lambeth Palace Library – Carew MSS
Leeds City Libraries – Port book of Derry
National Archives of Ireland – Copy of Strabane's charter, Lodge MSS
National Library of Ireland – Rich MSS
Public Record Office of Northern Ireland – Abercorn papers (D623); Groves
    collection (T808); Erne papers (D1939)
Trinity College, Dublin – Visitation Book of Ulster 1622

Printed primary sources

Calendar of the State Papers relating to Ireland – James I & Charles I
Calendar of the Patent Rolls of Ireland – James I & Charles I
The Civil Survey 1654–56 – R. C. Simington (ed.) (1937)
Maps of the escheated counties in Ireland, 1609 (1861)
Ulster and other Irish Maps c. 1600 – G. A. Hayes–McCoy (ed.) (1964)

Secondary sources

The Bishopric of Derry & Irish Society (vol. 1) – T. W. Moody & J. G.
 Simms (eds) (1968)

'The Survey of Armagh & Tyrone 1622' – V. Treadwell (ed), *Ulster Journal
 of Archaeology*, 3rd series (1964)

A History of the House of Hamilton – George Hamilton (1933)

An Historical Account of the Plantation in Ulster – George Hill (1877)

Indexes to Irish Wills (Derry and Raphoe) – Gertrude Thrift (ed.) (1920)

The Londonderry Plantation 1609–41 – T. W. Moody (1939)

The Making of Modern Ireland – J. C. Beckett (1966)

Notes on the Literary History of Strabane – A. A. Campbell (1902)

Scots Mercenary Forces in Ireland 1565–1603 – G. A. Hayes–McCoy (1937)

Tudor and Stuart Ireland – Margaret MacCurtain (1972)

Index

Where a number is followed by the letter p it indicates that the reference relates to an illustration